THE COUNT OF MONTE CRISTO

NOTES

including
- *Life of the Author*
- *Character Sketches*
- *Brief Plot Synopsis*
- *Summaries and Commentaries*
- *Suggested Essay Questions*
- *Select Bibliography*

by
James L. Roberts, Ph.D.
Dept. of English
University of Nebraska

Hungry Minds™

Best-Selling Books • Digital Downloads • e-Books • Answer Networks • e-Newsletters • Branded Web Sites • e-Learning
New York, NY • Cleveland, OH • Indianapolis, IN

CliffsNotes™ Dumas' *The Count Oof Monte Cristo*

Published by:
Hungry Minds, Inc.
909 Third Avenue
New York, NY 10022

www.hungryminds.com
www.cliffsnotes.com (CliffsNotes Web site)

ISBN: 0-8220-0326-0

Printed in the United States of America

10 9

1V/SV/QZ/QR/IN

Distributed in the United States by Hungry Minds, Inc.

Distributed by CDG Books Canada Inc. for Canada; by Transworld Publishers Limited in the United Kingdom; by IDG Norge Books for Norway; by IDG Sweden Books for Sweden; by IDG Books Australia Publishing Corporation Pty. Ltd. for Australia and New Zealand; by TransQuest Publishers Pte Ltd. for Singapore, Malaysia, Thailand, Indonesia, and Hong Kong; by Gotop Information Inc. for Taiwan; by ICG Muse, Inc. for Japan; by Norma Comunicaciones S.A. for Columbia; by Intersoft for South Africa; by Eyrolles for France; by International Thomson Publishing for Germany, Austria and Switzerland; by Distribuidora Cuspide for Argentina; by LR International for Brazil; by Galileo Libros for Chile; by Ediciones ZETA S.C.R. Ltda. for Peru; by WS Computer Publishing Corporation, Inc., for the Philippines; by Contemporanea de Ediciones for Venezuela; by Express Computer Distributors for the Caribbean and West Indies; by Micronesia Media Distributor, Inc. for Micronesia; by Grupo Editorial Norma S.A. for Guatemala; by Chips Computadoras S.A. de C.V. for Mexico; by Editorial Norma de Panama S.A. for Panama; by American Bookshops for Finland. Authorized Sales Agent: Anthony Rudkin Associates for the Middle East and North Africa.

For general information on Hungry Minds' products and services please contact our Customer Care department; within the U.S. at 800-762-2974, outside the U.S. at 317-572-3993 or fax 317-572-4002.

For sales inquiries and resellers information, including discounts, premium and bulk quantity sales and foreign language translations please contact our Customer Care department at 800-434-3422, fax 317-572-4002 or write to Hungry Minds, Inc., Attn: Customer Care department, 10475 Crosspoint Boulevard, Indianapolis, IN 46256.

For information on licensing foreign or domestic rights, please contact our Sub-Rights Customer Care department at 212-884-5000.

For information on using Hungry Minds' products and services in the classroom or for ordering examination copies, please contact our Educational Sales department at 800-434-2086 or fax 317-572-4005.

Please contact our Public Relations department at 212-884-5163 for press review copies or 212-884-5000 for author interviews and other publicity information or fax 212-884-5400.

For authorization to photocopy items for corporate, personal, or educational use, please contact Copyright Clearance Center, 222 Rosewood Drive, Danvers, MA 01923, or fax 978-750-4470.

Hungry Minds™ is a trademark of Hungry Minds, Inc.

CONTENTS

THE COUNT OF MONTE CRISTO
Notes

LIFE OF THE AUTHOR

Dumas, the author of *The Three Musketeers* and *The Count of Monte Cristo,* among scores of other novels, was born on July 24, 1802. His father was somewhat of an adventurer-soldier, a mulatto, and was not a favorite of Napoleon because of his staunch republicanism. Therefore, on his father's death in 1806, when Alexandre was only four, the family was left in rather severe financial straits. The young boy's formal education was scanty, most of it provided by a priest, and as soon as he could qualify, Alexandre entered the services of a lawyer. As he grew older, he became close friends with the son of an exiled Swedish nobleman, and the two of them began to dabble in vaudeville enterprises. Later, as a young man, Dumas went to Paris and secured a position as a clerk to the Duc d'Orleans; this was a marvelous stroke of good fortune, for the Duc would soon become king, and Dumas would write a superb *Memoir* about his many and varied mishaps while he was employed by the future king.

At the same time, Dumas and his old friend, Leuven, produced several melodramas. When he was twenty-two, however, a melodrama of his own making presented itself: Dumas found himself the father of an illegitimate son by a dressmaker, Marie Labay; when the boy was seven, Dumas went to court to get custody of him, and succeeded.

Professionally, this was an extremely happy time for Dumas; for six years, he and Leuven had been collaborating on plays, and their legitimate dramas had been staged to much popular acclaim. Then in 1829, Dumas' *Henri III et sa cour (Henry III and His Court)* was produced; it was Dumas' first spectacular triumph. The Duc was so fond of it that he appointed Dumas the librarian of the Palais Royal.

The Revolution of 1830 interrupted Dumas' playwriting, and for a pleasant and amusing account of these years, one should consult Dumas' *Memoirs* for many rich and humorous anecdotes (not worrying unduly about the degree of truth in them, of course). Then, because Dumas was implicated in some "irregularities" during a noted French general's funeral, he suddenly decided to "tour" Switzerland; as a result, we have another long series of delightful *Memoirs*, this time issued as travel books. It should be noted, though, that Dumas always retained his affectionate relationship with the Duc, and that he eventually returned to France, where he composed many first-rate, long-running plays.

Dumas' well-known collaboration with Auguste Maquet began in 1837 and resulted in a series of historical novels in which Dumas hoped to reconstruct the major events of French history. For example, the Three Musketeers are united in order to defend the honor of Anne of Austria against Richelieu. This particular novel in the series was so popular that Dumas immediately composed two sequels and, by coincidence, *The Count of Monte Cristo* was also written during this same period, with the help of collaborators.

In fact, Dumas, with the aid of collaborators, turned out so much fiction and miscellaneous writing that it has been remarked that "No one has ever read the whole of Dumas, not even himself." We know now, however, that Dumas' assistants only provided him with rough plotlines and suggested incidents to him. He himself filled in the outlines, and all of his novels' manuscripts are in his handwriting.

Like so many creative and productive men, Dumas' life ended in a series of personal and financial tragedies. He built a strangely beautiful and impressive French Gothic, English Renaissance hybrid mansion and filled it with a multitude of scavenger-friends; both home and hangers-on were tremendous drains on his purse, as was the construction and upkeep of his own theater, the Theatre Historique, built specifically for the performance of his own plays.

In 1851, Dumas moved to Brussels, as much for his political advantage as it was to escape creditors—despite the 1,200 volumes which bore his name—and he died not long after a scandalous liaison with an American circus girl, a situation that he might well have chosen as a fictional framework for his demise.

Dumas' son, Alexandre Dumas *fils*, is remembered today chiefly for his first novel, *The Lady of the Camellias*, which was the basis for the libretto of Verdi's opera *La Traviata*, as well as for the plot of one of Hollywood's classic films, *Camille*, starring Greta Garbo.

CHARACTER SKETCHES

The Count and His Friends

Edmond Dantès (alias the Count of Monte Cristo; his other aliases are Sinbad the Sailor, Abbé Busoni, and Lord Wilmore)

Dantès is the dashing and romantic hero of the novel; at the age of nineteen, he is falsely imprisoned for a crime which he did not commit and is kept in the horrible dungeon of the Chateau d'If, where he undergoes unbelievable hardships and sufferings that would destroy an ordinary man. While imprisoned, Dantès hears a fellow prisoner digging a tunnel, and so he too begins digging. When the two men finally meet, the other prisoner turns out to be a learned Abbé, who teaches Dantès many languages, sciences, history, and other subjects. They become as father and son, and when the Abbé is about to die, he reveals to Dantès the hiding place of a long-secret buried treasure, consisting of untold wealth in gold coins, diamonds, and other precious jewels.

After fourteen years of bitter imprisonment and hardships, and after a very daring and miraculous escape, Dantès is able to discover the buried treasure on the island of Monte Cristo, and so he buys the island. He becomes the Count of Monte Cristo and dedicates himself to becoming God's avenging angel. The rest of his life is spent, at first, performing acts of goodness and charity for the good people whom he has known. Then he devotes his life to bringing about God's retribution against the evil people who were responsible for his imprisonment. The largest portion of the novel deals with his unique methods of effecting this revenge against his enemies, who became, during Dantès' fourteen years of imprisonment, very powerful and very wealthy people.

Monsieur Dantès, *pere*

Edmond Dantès' old father, for whom he has a deep devotion – so deep, in fact, that part of the revenge which he takes against his enemies is due to the fact that their treatment of his father caused him to die of starvation. Likewise, those people, like Monsieur Morrel, who treated Dantès' father kindly when he was in despair, come into the good graces of Monte Cristo and are rewarded by him.

Monsieur Morrel, a shipbuilder and shipowner

This is a kindly man interested only in doing good for others and for his family. At the beginning of the novel, when the captain of one of his ships dies en route home, Monsieur Morrel is so impressed with the way that the young, nineteen-year-old Edmond Dantès takes over the captainship of the *Pharaon* that he makes him captain of the ship. This act causes the antagonism of others. Likewise, when Dantès is imprisoned, Monsieur Morrel risks his reputation by continually applying for Dantès' release, even though politically it is an extremely dangerous thing to do. When he learns of the death of Edmond Dantès' father, Morrel arranges the proper ceremonies. Later, upon learning about these facts, the Count of Monte Cristo is able to return the favors triple-fold, for not only does he save Monsieur Morrel's life, but he is able to recover Monsieur Morrel's fortune.

Julie Morrel Herbault

Monsieur Morrel's daughter, who first meets the Count of Monte Cristo as "Sinbad the Sailor"; he sends her on an errand to obtain monies which will save her father's business.

Maximilien Morrel

The son of Monsieur Morrel who will later become not merely a close young friend of the Count of Monte Cristo, but because of his nobility of soul and his devotion and loyalty, he will become the Count of Monte Cristo's spiritual "son" and the recipient of a great deal of the Count's fortune. Thus, virtue is highly rewarded.

Cloclès

A long-time employee in the Morrel firm who remains loyal to the firm, despite its financial difficulties.

Abbé Faria

The wise, learned, and lovable political prisoner in the Chateau d'If; he is a remarkable and ingenious person, capable of creating some digging tools out of virtually nothing. He writes the life history of a noble Italian family, the Spada family (who possessed such great wealth that, after the family suffered poisoning, their fabulous treasure remained hidden for centuries until the Abbé Faria was able to decipher the secret message giving the location of this treasure, which Faria, in turn, reveals to Dantès). Faria becomes Dantès' spiritual "father" and teaches Dantès not only worldly matters of languages, science, and mathematics, but also spiritual matters. His death in the Chateau d'If provides Dantès with his daring means of escape.

Cesare Spada

A member of the Spada family living in Italy in the fourteenth century; he amassed such a huge fortune that the expression "rich as Spada" became a common saying, thus evoking much envy for such great wealth. Spada was poisoned – but not before he secretly buried his great wealth on the island of Monte Cristo. Centuries later, the Abbé Faria worked as secretary to the last surviving member of the family, Cardinal Spada, who still possessed a breviary with some papers dating back to the fourteenth century. When Abbé Faria was writing a history of the family, he discovered the clues which led him to the whereabouts of the secret treasure that later becomes the source of great wealth for Dantès, the Count of Monte Cristo.

Haydée

This is the daughter of the Ali Pasha, whom Fernand, alias Baron de Morcerf, betrayed and sold into slavery. She became the "property" of the Count of Monte Cristo. At Morcerf's trial, she is able to testify as to Morcerf's villainy and thus convict him. Eventually, Monte Cristo begins to fall in love with her and at the end of the novel, they sail off into the horizon: "On the dark blue line separating the sky from the Mediterranean," the white sail carries the Count and Haydée away.

Bertuccio

Early in his life, Bertuccio had been betrayed by Villefort, when he requested punishment for the murderer of his brother, and Villefort, having no respect for Bertuccio's Corsican heritage, ignored Bertuccio's request. This refusal prompted Bertuccio to swear a vendetta against Villefort. Some years later, Bertuccio traced Villefort to the Chateau of the Saint-Mérans, where Villefort was burying alive his and a lady's child (the lady will later be revealed to be the Baroness Danglars). After stabbing Villefort and thinking that he killed him, Bertuccio took the box, assuming that it contained money or gold or something else valuable. To his dismay, a live infant was inside, whom Bertuccio took home to his sister-in-law. The woman raised the child and called him Benedetto; later, his alias is Andrea Cavalcanti.

Bertuccio was involved in a smuggling ring which used Caderousse's inn as a hiding place. One time, Bertuccio was hiding in Caderousse's inn when he overheard the story about Abbé Busoni (alias Monte Cristo) giving Caderousse a diamond; Caderousse sold the diamond, then killed the diamond merchant and his own wife. Bertuccio was falsely arrested for the murders, and he pleaded with the judge to find Abbé Busoni, who could verify his story.

A search was made and eventually, Abbé Busoni came to the prison, listened to Bertuccio's confession, including the details about his alleged murder of Villefort. Abbé Busoni managed to free Bertuccio and recommended that he enter the employment of the Count of Monte Cristo. Thus, when the Count takes Bertuccio to the Chateau of the Saint-Mérans, he knows from Bertuccio's confession to Abbé Busoni that this is the place where Bertuccio attempted to murder Villefort, and therefore, he extracts yet another confession, which is identical to the first. For Monte Cristo, this is proof that he has Bertuccio's total allegiance.

Luigi Vampa

Chief of a large gang of bandits, whose headquarters are in the ancient catacombs outside of Rome. Some years earlier, Monte Cristo met Vampa when the bandit was still a young shepherd, and they exchanged gifts which should have made them lifelong friends, but apparently Vampa forgot because he later tried to capture the Count only to be captured *by* the Count. The Count could have turned Vampa over to "Roman justice," which would have quickly snuffed out his life, but instead, the two men parted friends, with the condition that

Vampa and his band would always respect the Count and all of the Count's friends – this is how the Count was able to so easily rescue Albert de Morcerf. Of course, there is always the suspicion (or knowledge) that the Count "arranged" the kidnapping in the first place, so as to make Albert indebted to him, because it is through Albert's obligations that the Count will be introduced to all of his enemies in Paris, including Albert's father, who betrayed Edmond Dantès many years ago. Vampa also serves the Count by kidnapping Monsieur Danglars at the end of the novel and holding him prisoner until the Baron is forced to spend all of the five million francs that he embezzled from charity hospitals. Again, every indication points to the Count of Monte Cristo's arranging the kidnapping, thus effecting his final revenge against Danglars.

Signor Pastrini

The owner of the Hotel de Londres in Rome who arranges for the meeting between the Count of Monte Cristo and Albert de Morcerf, a meeting which the Count anticipates so that his introduction to his enemies can be effected.

Peppino

An agent of Luigi Vampa, he is deeply indebted to the Count of Monte Cristo for saving his life. Peppino was sentenced to death, and the Count used his wealth (he gave one of the three enormous emeralds from his treasures to the Pope, who installed it in his tiara) and his influence to buy a pardon for Peppino, just minutes before Peppino was to be executed.

Ali, the Count's mute Nubian valet

He serves virtually no function in the novel except to lasso Madame de Villefort's runaway horses, thus obligating the Villeforts to the Count.

Jacopo

Dantès first meets Jacopo when he escapes from the Chateau d'If. Swimming toward a ship which he hopes will rescue him, he is approaching the vessel when his strength gives out. He is pulled out of the water by Jacopo, who then lends him a pair of pants and a shirt. Thus, Monte Cristo is indebted to Jacopo for saving his life and is symbolically aligned with him by sharing Jacopo's clothes.

Later, when Monte Cristo pretends to be wounded on the island of Monte Cristo, Jacopo proves his devotion and loyalty to the Count by volunteering to give up his share of the smuggling bounty in order to look after his friend. Thus, Monte Cristo now knows that he has found a loyal and devoted friend whom he can fully trust to help him once he has recovered the treasure of the Spada family. Later, Jacopo is fully rewarded for his loyalty to the Count by being made, among other things, the captain of Monte Cristo's private yacht.

Enemies of the Count (and their families and friends)

Gaspard Caderousse

He is one of the original conspirators who falsified facts in a letter and thereby framed Edmond Dantès. He never came to Dantès' aid when he was imprisoned, and later, the Count of Monte Cristo comes to him disguised as the Abbé Busoni and learns about the entire nature of Caderousse's conspiracy against Dantès, as well as Caderousse's rampant duplicity. Busoni rewards Caderousse for his narration, hoping that Caderousse will become an honest man. However, Caderousse's greed is too strong, and he continues to rob and murder until one evening, while attempting to rob the Count's house, he is killed by an accomplice, just as the Count reveals that he is Edmond Dantès.

Monsieur de Villefort

Villefort is described early in the novel as the type of person who "would sacrifice anything to his ambition, even his own father." And throughout the novel, whenever political expediency demands it, he denies his own father, who was a Bonapartist and therefore opposed to the ruling royalty. When it is discovered that Edmond Dantès has a letter from the island of Elba, where Napoleon is confined, to be delivered to Villefort's father (Monsieur Noirtier), Villefort, in order to protect his own interest, has Dantès imprisoned in the impregnable fortress of the Chateau d'If, from which there is no escape. (Villefort is the prosecuting attorney, with great powers of life and death.) In addition, Villefort closes his ears to the entreaties of the elder Dantès, as well as to Monsieur Morrel, who tries on several occasions to plead for Dantès' release.

Because of his political ambitions, Villefort is willing to have an innocent man imprisoned for life. Thus, he becomes the central enemy against whom the Count of Monte Cristo effects revenge. During Dantès' fourteen years of imprisonment, Villefort uses all sorts of conniving means to achieve the powerful post of Deputy Minister of France; he becomes the most powerful law enforcement man in the nation. He has also made a politically advantageous marriage to the daughter of the Marquis and Marquise de Saint-Méran and has one daughter, Valentine, by that marriage. He later takes a second wife and has one son, Edouard, by her. He also has had an affair with a woman who becomes the Baroness Danglars, and Villefort uses his wife's family mansion (Monte Cristo later purchases this mansion) to conceal his mistress (the woman who will become Madame Danglars) while she is pregnant. When the child is born, Villefort announces that the child is stillborn and takes the child in a box to the garden, where he plans to bury him alive. However, an assassin who has a vendetta for Villefort stabs him and, thinking that the box contains treasure, he takes it, only to find that it contains an infant who is ultimately raised by him and his sister-in-law. The boy is named Benedetto, and he will later be brought back to Paris by Monte Cristo as Prince Cavalcanti and will accuse his own father, Villefort, of all of his dastardly deeds. This is part of Monte Cristo's revenge: a son whom the father tried to kill as an infant becomes the instrument of Divine Justice and accuses and destroys the evil father.

Renée, the first Madame de Villefort, née Mademoiselle Saint-Méran

The mother of Valentine. Her marriage to Villefort was "politically" arranged, and she does not appear in the novel.

Valentine de Villefort

Valentine is the daughter of the first Madame de Villefort and is, therefore, the granddaughter of the Marquis and Marquise de

Saint-Méran, whose fortune she is due to inherit. This fortune causes extreme envy in her stepmother. Valentine, like her brother, Edouard, and Albert de Morcerf and Eugénie Danglars represent the innocent persons who are trapped by the evil machinations of one or both parents. Valentine's mother, as far as we know, was an innocent person, and Valentine herself represents the absolute purity of young womanhood who will attract the pure love of the noble Maximilien Morrel. She unknowingly also attracts the enmity of her wicked stepmother, who tries to poison her. Since it is the Count of Monte Cristo who recognizes the stepmother's envy and greed and because he instructs her in the use of poison, the Count undergoes his greatest change as a result of his exposure to some of the children of his enemies. Prior to the realization that his beloved friend, Maximilien, loves Valentine, The Count had begun his revenge with the biblical philosophy that the sins of the father will be visited upon the later generations, even unto the fourth generation. Therefore, he is not concerned that Valentine's stepmother might poison her; this would be proper punishment for the wicked father. It is only when Maximilien Morrel reveals that Valentine is his true love that the Count undergoes a significant change of heart, and because of the Count's love for Maximilien, he sets a plot in motion that will save the life of the daughter of his most hated enemy. To do so, however, he must ask her to undergo such tremendous terrors as being entombed alive, until she is reborn into happiness with Maximilien at the end of the novel.

Héloïse, the second Madame de Villefort

Early in the novel, in Paris, the Count of Monte Cristo became acquainted with Madame de Villefort, and in an intimate conversation, he discussed with her his extensive knowledge of poisons, particularly a poison known as "brucine" which, taken in small doses, can cure a person but which, taken in larger doses, will kill one. Since Madame de Villefort has a child named Edouard, she becomes insanely jealous of the large fortune which her stepdaughter, Valentine, will inherit from the Marquis and Marquise de Saint-Méran. Likewise, Valentine is to inherit most of Monsieur Noirtier's fortune, making her one of the wealthiest heiresses in France. In Madame de Villefort's desire to possess the wealth that Valentine is to inherit, she poisons both the Marquis and the Marquise (and during the process, one of the servants, Barrois), and then she believes that she has also successfully poisoned Valentine. Later, when her husband accuses her of the poisonings and demands that she commit suicide or else face public execution, she poisons both herself and their nine-year-old son, leaving Villefort totally distraught. Thus, the Count's revenge is complete against the cruel and inhuman Monsieur de Villefort.

Edouard de Villefort

The young nine-year-old son of the second Madame de Villefort and her husband. He is merely an innocent pawn caught in a vicious power struggle. The death of this innocent young boy causes the Count of Monte Cristo to re-evaluate his belief in the rightness of the "sins of the father being visited upon the son." The Count feels deep remorse over the death of the young boy, and he tries to save his life, but on failing to do so, he places the innocent, dead boy beside the body of his dead mother.

Monsieur Noirtier

Villefort's very strong-willed father, who is the source of great embarrassment to Villefort and a threat to his ambitions. Monsieur Noirtier was one of France's leading Bonapartists (supporters of Napoleon), and his political views, his power in the Bonapartist party, and his influence make him a thorn in the side of his son, an opportunist who is willing to support whichever political party is in power. It is because of a letter carried by Edmond Dantès and addressed to Monsieur Noirtier and sent from someone on the Isle of Elba (probably Napoleon himself), that Villefort is persuaded to imprison Edmond Dantès so that no royalists (supporters of the king) will ever know that Villefort's father is so intimately associated with Napoleon. Later in the novel, when Monsieur Noirtier is paralyzed, he is able to communicate only with his servant, Barrois, and with his beloved granddaughter, Valentine, whom he tries to warn about the intricate plots surrounding her because of her pending inheritance.

Monsieur Danglars, later Baron Danglars

When we first meet this envious and devious man, we are immediately aware that he has a jealous hatred for Edmond Dantès simply because Dantès is younger, more capable, more assured, and self-confident and because he is a thoroughly good-natured young man of nineteen, with complete openness, honesty, and frankness. Danglars is the one who conceives of the conspiracy against Dantès, and he is the one responsible for writing the treacherous, anonymous note which sends Dantès to prison for fourteen years. The note and the handwriting are permanently engraved in Dantès' eyes, and years later, he is able to confirm Danglars' evil duplicity by another sample of his handwriting, in addition to the somewhat reliable testimony which Caderousse tells to the Abbé Busoni, an alias for the Count of Monte Cristo. By various illegal means, Danglars first ingratiates himself into the family of a prominent banker, later marries the banker's widow, and by using illegal banking methods, he quickly becomes an extremely wealthy man. The Count of Monte Cristo, however, is even more clever, and he gradually involves himself in Danglars' finances to the point that Danglars eventually goes bankrupt. But he does manage to confiscate five million francs in bank notes, and he flees to Italy, hoping to have them cashed. He is captured by the bandit chief Luigi Vampa, an old friend of the Count of Monte Cristo, and then he is gradually stripped of all his five million francs. He is finally freed by the bandits, but he is now an old and broken man, and, worst of all, he is penniless. The Count's vengeance has at last been effected.

Baroness Danglars

She is the wife of Danglars, but they have lived separate lives for over seven years, and both have their own separate lovers. At present, her lover is Lucien Debray, an officer in Baron Danglars' banking establishment, who is collaborating with her to manipulate stocks and bonds so that they can accumulate large sums of money. When their scheme is over, because Danglars is on the verge of bankruptcy, young Lucien divides the money and then drops Madame Danglars as his mistress. Madame Danglars also figures prominently in another aspect of the plot. Earlier, she had an affair with Monsieur Villefort, the Count's archenemy, and she retired to Villefort's wife's family estate to have their child in secrecy. The estate is later purchased by the Count of Monte Cristo, and her son, whom she thought to be dead, is paid by the Count of Monte Cristo to pretend to be the wealthy

Prince Cavalcanti. As such, her illegitimate son becomes engaged to her own legitimate daughter, Eugénie.

Eugénie Danglars

The daughter who is first engaged to Albert de Morcerf and then, in another arranged marriage, to the bogus Prince Cavalcanti, alias the criminal Benedetto, who is actually her mother's illegitimate son. She abhors the idea of marriage and bondage and wants to live as a liberated woman in charge of her own destiny. When her fiancé is exposed as a fraud and a murderer, she and a girl friend escape; they hope to reach Rome by a circuitous route. Her disappearance is one of the final blows to the pride of her villainous father.

Fernand Mondego, alias the Count de Morcerf

In his youth, Fernand was a simple fisherman and a sometime smuggler who was in love with the woman whom Edmond Dantès was engaged to, Mercédès Herrera. Because Mercédès loved Fernand as a brother, Edmond Dantès trusted him. However, it is Fernand who actually mailed the letter condemning Dantès, hoping all the while that if Dantès was arrested, he would then be able to marry Mercédès. By evil means, he was able to use his smuggling skills and his treachery in warfare to eventually be made a Count and awarded an immense sum of money. Sometime during his rise to power, he married Mercédès, who had waited a long time for Dantès, but finally abandoned hope. Fernand gained most of his wealth by betraying a high authority named Ali Pasha, whose daughter he sold into slavery, and who is now the paramour of the Count of Monte Cristo. When all of his treachery is exposed and he discovers that his wife and son have deserted him, Fernand shoots himself.

Mercédès Herrera, later the Countess de Morcerf

She is the innocent victim of many of the above machinations. She loved only Edmond Dantès, and when he seemingly disappeared forever, she attempted to care for his father. When the elderly Dantès died, she had no place to go, and so she succumbed to pressure and married Fernand. As the Countess de Morcerf, she became an educated and distinguished but unhappy woman. She is the only person who knows that the Count of Monte Cristo is really Edmond Dantès. When she discovers the full extent of her husband's treachery, she leaves his house without any of his wealth (giving all her money to charity hospitals), and she returns to the small house which once belonged to Edmond Dantès' father, there to live out her life in deep prayer.

Albert de Morcerf

When the young Viscount Albert was visiting Rome, he happened to be staying in the same hotel where the Count of Monte Cristo was staying. They became close acquaintances, and when Albert was kidnapped by a gang of bandits, whose chief was Luigi Vampa, a man deeply indebted to the Count of Monte Cristo, the Count was able to rescue Albert before the bandits put him to death. Thus, young Albert was indebted to Monte Cristo forever for saving his life. Because of Albert's obligation to him, the Count was later able to be introduced to all of his enemies in Paris, including Albert's father, Count de Morcerf (alias Fernand), who betrayed Dantès many years ago. Albert, however, apparently inherited all of his mother's goodness and none of his father's treachery. Eventually, Albert wins the love and respect of the Count of Monte Cristo, and even though the Count is on the verge of killing Albert in a duel after he is challenged and insulted by Albert, the Count's willingness to recognize Albert's goodness is another example of "an exception" to his belief in the "sons of the father rightly inheriting their father's guilt."

Benedetto, alias Andrea Cavalcanti

Being the illegitimate son of the immoral Madame Danglars and the corrupt, ambitious, and despicable Villefort, Benedetto represents almost pure evil. It is only by luck that he was not buried alive as an infant, but as his father, Villefort, was about to bury him, Bertuccio saw the box that Benedetto was in and mistakenly believed it to be filled with treasure. Bertuccio hoped to revenge himself on Villefort, and so he stabbed him and took the baby to his sister-in-law. Benedetto lived with her and made her life miserable. Then one day, he tied her up, beat her, and stole all of her money. Later, he was caught and found himself in prison, with Caderousse as a cellmate. By the time of the story, Monte Cristo has tracked him down and has paid him to disguise himself as a wealthy Italian nobleman so that he can use Benedetto in his larger, ultimate plan for total revenge against the traitorous Baron Danglars (by having him become engaged to Eugénie Danglars) and by exposing Villefort as the would-be murderer of his own infant son.

The Marquis and the Marquise de Saint-Méran

The first in-laws of Villefort, whose granddaughter, Valentine, will be the sole inheritor of their fortune, thus arousing the envy of the second Madame de Villefort, who poisons both the Marquis and the Marquise so that Valentine can inherit their fortune immediately and she can then poison Valentine, insuring that Edouard, Valentine's half-brother, will come into an immense fortune.

Monsieur de Boville

He is the Director of Prisons, from whom Dantès buys financial notes which are invested in Monsieur Morrel's shipping firm. Dantès is also able to secretly extract Villefort's note condemning him to what Villefort believed would be a life of isolated imprisonment. Boville is also involved in devastating financial transactions with Danglars.

Doctor d'Avrigny

The attending physician to the Villeforts, who is convinced that the Marquis and the Marquise de Saint-Méran were poisoned. After the death of Barrois, whom the doctor is certain was the victim of the same poison, he threatens Villefort with a police investigation, but is persuaded to keep the matter quiet. With Valentine's "seeming" death, d'Avrigny joins Maximilien in demanding punishment for the "supposed" murderer.

Lucien Debray

A young man in Monsieur Danglars' office who is having an affair with Madame Danglars; Debray and Madame Danglars are using certain information to destroy Danglars' fortune while increasing their own fortune tremendously.

Franz d'Epinay

One of the many men about town; he is a friend of Albert de Morcerf. Franz accompanies Albert to Rome, where he acts as an emissary between the bandits and Monte Cristo after Albert is captured by the bandits.

BRIEF PLOT SYNOPSIS

Edmond Dantès, a handsome, promising young sailor, skillfully docks the three-masted French ship, the *Pharaon,* in Marseilles after its captain died en route home. As a reward, Dantès is promised a captainship, but before he can claim his new post and be married to his fiancée, Mercédès, a conspiracy of four jealous and unsavory men arrange for him to be seized and secretly imprisoned in solitary confinement in the infamous Chateau d'If, a prison from which no one has ever escaped. The four men responsible are:

1. Fernand Mondego, who is jealous of Mercédès' love for Dantès;
2. Danglars, the purser of the *Pharaon,* who covets Dantès' promised captainship;
3. Caderousse, an unprincipled neighbor; and
4. Villefort, a prosecutor who knows that Dantès is carrying a letter addressed to Villefort's father; the old man is a Bonapartist who would probably be imprisoned by the present royalist regime were it not for his son's, Villefort's, influence. Villefort fears, however, that this letter might damage his own position, and so he makes sure, he thinks, that no one ever hears about either Dantès or the letter again.

For many years, Dantès barely exists in his tiny, isolated cell; he almost loses his mind and his will to live until one day he hears a fellow prisoner burrowing nearby. He too begins digging, and soon he meets an old Abbé who knows the whereabouts of an immense fortune, one that used to belong to an immensely wealthy Italian family.

Dantès and the Abbé continue digging for several years, and from the Abbé, Dantès learns history, literature, science, and languages, but when at last they are almost free, the Abbé dies. Dantès hides his body, then sews himself in the Abbé's burial sack. The guards arrive, carry the sack outside, and heave the body far out to sea.

Dantès manages to escape and is picked up by a shipful of smugglers, whom he joins until he can locate the island where the treasure is hidden. When he finally discovers it, he is staggered by the immensity of its wealth. And when he emerges into society again, he is the very rich and very handsome Count of Monte Cristo.

Monte Cristo has two goals – to reward those who were kind to him and his aging father, and to punish those responsible for his imprisonment. For the latter, he plans slow and painful punishment. To have spent fourteen years barely subsisting in a dungeon demands cruel and prolonged punishment.

As Monte Cristo, Dantès ingeniously manages to be introduced to the cream of Parisian society, among whom he goes unrecognized. But Monte Cristo, in contrast, recognizes *all* of his enemies – all now wealthy and influential men.

Fernand has married Mercédès and is now known as Count de Morcerf. Monte Cristo releases information to the press that proves that Morcerf is a traitor, and Morcerf is ruined socially. Then Monte Cristo destroys Morcerf's relationship with his family, whom he adores. When they leave him, he is so distraught that he shoots himself.

To revenge himself on Danglars, who loves money more than anything else, Monte Cristo ruins him financially.

To revenge himself on Caderousse, Monte Cristo easily traps Caderousse because of his insatiable greed, then watches as one of Caderousse's cohorts murders him.

To revenge himself on Villefort, Monte Cristo slowly reveals to Villefort that he knows about a love affair that Villefort had long ago with the present Madame Danglars. He also reveals to him, by hints, that he knows about an illegitimate child whom he fathered, a child whom Villefort believed that he buried alive. The child lived, however, and is now engaged to Danglars' daughter, who is the illegitimate young man's half-sister.

Ironically, Villefort's wife proves to be even more villainous than her husband, for she poisons the parents of Villefort's first wife; then she believes that she has successfully poisoned her husband's daughter by his first marriage. With those people dead, her own son is in line for an enormous inheritance. Villefort, however, discovers his wife's plottings and threatens her, and so she poisons herself and their son.

At this point, Dantès is half-fearful that his revenge has been too thorough, but because he is able to unite two young people who are very much in love and unite them on the Isle of Monte Cristo, he sails away, happy and satisfied, never to be seen again.

SUMMARIES AND COMMENTARIES

Chapters 1–6*

ACCUSATION AND ARREST

Summary

The time: February, 1815. The place: Marseilles, France. The *Pharaon,* a three-masted sailing ship coming from Italy, is docking. Like all dockings, this one attracts a large crowd, but this particular ship draws a great crowd because it belongs to a wealthy man of Marseilles, Monsieur Morrel. Strangely, there is a quiet, solemn air about the approaching ship, even though the pilot seems to have her in perfect control. Suddenly, we see a man being rowed out to the ship, where he hails a tall, dark, and slender young man, Edmond Dantès, on board the *Pharaon.* The man in the rowboat is Monsieur Morrel, the ship's owner, and he inquires about the gloomy mood of the sailors; he is told that their captain died of brain fever, but that the cargo is safe. The handsome young man then gives orders to lower the top sails and invites Morrel aboard. Monsieur Danglars, the purser, comes forward to give Morrel further information about the voyage.

Danglars, a rather melancholy, oily man of about twenty-five, laments the loss of the ship's captain, a man who spent his life at sea. Morrel remarks that a life at sea doesn't necessarily guarantee one's worth as a sailor; he cites young Dantès' obvious skill and relish for sailoring. Danglars' face darkens. Dantès, he says, took command of the ship with no authority and then lingered a day at the Isle of Elba instead of sailing on a straight course for Marseilles. Morrel calls to Dantès and asks him if this is true. Dantès explains that he was carry-

---

*Chapter divisions correspond to Lowell Bair's translation: Bantam Books, 1956.

ing out an order of the late Captain Leclère – to deliver a package to a Marshal Bertrand.

Whispering, Morrel asks Dantès about the health of Napoleon, and Dantès explains that Napoleon inquired about the ship and its cargo and that he was pleased to discover that the ship belonged to Morrel. This news pleases Morrel, and he praises Dantès for stopping at Elba. But he warns him to tell no one about the parcel which he delivered. Dantès then leaves to greet a customs officer, and Danglars steps forward, criticizing the handsome young Dantès and asking Morrel about a letter which the captain gave Dantès along with the packet. Sharply, Morrel asks Danglars how *he* knew about the packet. Danglars tries to explain, but it is obvious that he was eavesdropping; thus, he hastily excuses himself and says that he was wrong to even mention the letter.

Morrel invites Dantès to dinner, but the young man cannot accept; his father awaits him, as does his fiancée, Mercédès. Morrel asks Dantès about Leclère's letter, and the sailor is puzzled. Leclére, he says, was "unable to write."

Then he asks for two weeks' leave – to be married and to go to Paris. He is granted the request; moreover, says Morrel, Dantès shall be the new captain of the *Pharaon* when he returns from Paris – that is, if Morrel can convince his partner to agree to the captainship. Morrel then questions Dantès about the character of Danglars, the purser of the *Pharaon,* and Dantès' answer is immediate: Danglars is no friend of his; however, as a purser, he is quite satisfactory, and if Morrel is satisfied with Danglars, then Dantès will respect the purser.

At home, Dantès' sudden appearance causes his father to go terribly pale. Dantès, in contrast, is exultant! He is a captain at nineteen, with a large salary, plus a share in the profits, and he is soon going to be married to the woman he adores! Noticing that his father is obviously very weak, he discovers that his father has very little money. Dantès had left with a debt to Caderousse, a neighbor, and after Dantès sailed, Caderousse demanded full payment, which amounted to almost the full sum that Dantès left for his father.

Caderousse enters, hoping to gain information about Dantès' new post and also to mock Dantès for refusing to flatter Morrel and accept his invitation to dinner. Dantès, however, dismisses Caderousse's criticism and hurries off to see his fiancée, wincing that Caderousse once did the family a great favor long ago. Caderousse leaves, meets

Danglars, and the two men go to a tavern to drink wine and speculate about Dantès' future.

Not far away is the village of the Catalans, a community of closely knit Spanish people living near Marseilles. Mercédès lives in this village, and at present, Fernand, a young man from her village, is trying to convince her to marry him. Mercédès is frank with him, declaring her love for Dantès, but Fernand begs her to marry him instead. Dantès appears, and he and Mercédès fall into each other's arms. Fernand leaves and is stopped by Danglars and Caderousse. They invite him for a drink and then make him drunk with wine and thoughts of revenge. Dantès and Mercédès pass the tavern, and Dantès is so happy that he invites all three men to his wedding. After the wedding, he reveals, he must go to Paris to deliver a letter which he received on Elba. Danglars is overjoyed with this news; a plot to foil Dantès' promise of happiness begins to form.

Next day, Dantès' official appointment as captain of the *Pharaon* is made in the tavern amidst much celebrating. But when the thunder of three loud knocks is heard, all is quiet. Four armed soldiers and a corporal enter. Dantès is arrested – with no explanation.

Meanwhile, in one of the aristocratic residences of Marseilles, another betrothal is being celebrated by several enemies of Napoleon. At the center of this scene is Monsieur de Villefort, who describes Napoleon as *more* than a man; he was, Villefort says, a symbol, the personification of equality. Those assembled are obviously royalists, and they chide Villefort about his attitude toward Napoleon. Villefort flashes with anger: his *father* may be a Bonapartist, but *he himself* is the antithesis of his father.

At that moment, a servant enters and whispers that a Bonapartist plot has been discovered: Edmond Dantès has been charged as the traitor responsible for delivering correspondence between "the usurper" and the Bonapartist party of Paris.

Villefort leaves to question Dantès, and at the police commission, he meets Morrel, who pleads Dantès' innocence, which is unnecessary, for as Villefort questions Dantès, he sees that the young man is utterly candid and frank – and innocent. Villefort gives Dantès the accusatory note; Dantès, he says, has jealous and dangerous enemies. Dantès then tells Villefort that the letter was entrusted to him to give to a certain Monsieur Noirtier. Villefort pales; Noirtier is his father. He makes Dantès swear that no one knows the contents of the letter, then he apparently frees him, hoping fervently that no one can link him, Villefort, with any traitorous plot of his father's.

Dantès leaves, but instead of being escorted to freedom, he is shut behind the iron doors of a prison. A police van then comes for him, and he is placed in a boat, despite his protests. He is rowed to the Chateau d'If, an infamous prison because of its brutality and its impossibility of escape, and then he is taken to the dungeon, where they throw "madmen with madmen."

Commentary

The greatness and the enduring popularity of *The Count of Monte Cristo* is mainly accounted for by the narrative force of the novel. In very simple terms, the novel tells an exciting story in an engaging and straightforward narrative – a narrative that grasps and involves the reader in the action. This novel is, in literary terms, a "well-made Romantic adventure story." By "well-made," we mean that very early in the novel, Dumas sets up his characters, even though they are one-dimensional and predictable, and places them in situations where their actions are such that the reader will respond to them with sympathy or with revulsion and dislike. Thus, in the opening scenes, Danglars is presented as a troublemaker, a jealous and envious person for no other reason than pure jealousy and spite. He makes all sorts of false insinuations against Dantès in order to disgustingly ingratiate himself before the owner of the ship, Monsieur Morrel. In contrast to Danglars' sniveling and sycophantish behavior, Dantès is open and aboveboard in all his dealings. He immediately evokes trust in everyone except the envious Danglars, and it is Dantès' excellent qualities which win the complete confidence of the shipowner Morrel; in fact, as we learn later, Dantès has won the total allegiance of Monsieur Morrel, for he will risk his business in order to intercede for the imprisoned Dantès.

In the "well-made novel," we are immediately attracted to the hero and are likewise repulsed by people like Danglars and his cohort, Caderousse, the dishonorable neighbor who forced Dantès' old father into virtual starvation by demanding the return of a loan which Caderousse had made to Dantès. Early in the novel, therefore, the forces of good are aligned against the forces of evil and destruction. And in this alignment, Mercédès' friend Fernand becomes a willing partner in the conspiracy to frame Dantès (Fernand mails the accusatory letter), and, consequently, in these first six chapters, we have met all four enemies (Danglars, Caderousse, Fernand, and Villefort), against whom Dantès will ultimately seek revenge for his fourteen years of imprisonment.

By the term "Romantic," we mean a novel that is filled with high adventure, one in which the hero possesses the most noble of qualities and where he is often put to various tests and survives these tests superbly. It is a novel that does not focus on intricate character analysis, but emphasizes, instead, the narrative plot element, and the success of this type of novel is measured by how much it engages or captures the reader's interest in the adventures set forth.

In the first six chapters, Dumas has created his main character, or hero, has shown his superb qualities and capabilities, has presented him as a loyal friend to the late captain and as an honorable man of his word. Dumas has involved his character innocently in a political intrigue about which Dantès knows nothing. Furthermore, he is exposed to an overly ambitious official, Monsieur Villefort, who "would sacrifice anything to his ambitions, even his own father"; in addition, Villefort marries a woman whom he doesn't love in order to advance his financial and political future, and Villefort also uses Dantès as another instrument to further his career when he lies to the king that Dantès is a dangerous rebel involved in a treasonous plot against the king. These false accusations and political concerns cause Dantès to be sentenced to life imprisonment in the infamous Chateau d'If, a fortress legendary for its severe punishment and for its impossibility of escape. Until the time of this story, no prisoner had ever successfully escaped from this fortress, therefore making Dantès' escape a feat of great daring and magnitude.

The reader, of course, responds emotionally to Dantès' plight. While we do not now know who the author of the note is, we can assume that the jealous and spiteful Danglars is the perpetrator since he is the only person to know about the letter which Dantès was to deliver to Monsieur Noirtier. And ironically, if the letter had not been addressed to Villefort's father, an avid Bonapartist, then Villefort, a royalist, would not have used Dantès so badly, but Villefort's ambitions force him to remove anyone who might influence his desperate desire to rise to power. If Dantès knows the contents of the letter, or even the name of the addressee, then Villefort knows that he will be "ruined, ruined forever." Therefore, it is absolutely necessary to do away with Dantès forever, and thus by the end of the sixth chapter, the noble

Dantès is falsely imprisoned with no hope of escape and no hope of making contact with anyone in the outer world. In a rather catatonic state, he argues with a guard in the prison, and as a result, he is placed in a dungeon. These first six chapters, then, have shown the hero to be a person of potential greatness and honor being reduced to a hopeless prisoner with no hope for release and no contact with the outer world.

Chapters 7 – 12

DANTÈS' IMPRISONMENT

Summary

In his study at the Tuileries in Paris, King Louis XVIII jokes about Bonaparte's partisans causing "trouble" in the south of France – that is, he jokes about it until Villefort's arrival is announced. Villefort brings news of "dire importance" about a traitorous conspiracy: Napoleon has manned three ships, has left Elba, and is undoubtedly sailing for France. Villefort, carefully avoiding all names, says that he learned of this plot from a man (Dantès) whom he immediately ordered to be arrested when he learned that this man planned to carry a message to a dangerous Bonapartist in Paris (actually, Villefort's own father).

At that moment, the Minister of Police arrives and announces that Bonaparte landed near Antibes two days ago and is now marching on Paris. Louis is so angered that he is unable to speak, but in gratitude, he removes the Legion of Honor cross from around his neck and bestows it on Villefort because of Villefort's patriotic zeal. Later, and not without a little envy, the Minister of Police comments that Villefort has made "a magnificent beginning," and that his "fortune is assured." Villefort, we gather, is already impatient for the promising future that seemingly lies ahead for him.

Napoleon returns to France, ousts Louis, and begins what will be his Court of the Hundred Days. Normally, Villefort would probably have suffered the same fate as King Louis, but because of the influence of Villefort's father at Napoleon's court, Villefort retains his post. When Napoleon is defeated at Waterloo and Louis returns to the throne, Villefort is able to use his own influence to reinstate himself politically, and he decides to marry a woman whose family will further his political ambitions.

Meanwhile, Dantès remains a prisoner and knows nothing about Napoleon's return and his crushing defeat, or about Louis' return to Paris. Mercédès lives in absolute despair and is saved from suicide only because of her strong faith. Likewise, Dantès himself so despairs of ever gaining freedom that, finally, he too is on the brink of suicide. All hope seems to be absolutely denied to him. Thus, he decides to starve himself to death.

It is while Dantès is numb with hunger and illness that he hears a curious, animal-like scratching outside his cell, within the earth or within the foundations of the prison. It is not rats, he discovers; it is the famous old "mad Abbé Faria," who, it is believed, knows the location of a fabulous treasure. The Abbé has been imprisoned for twelve years and now believes that he will finally be able to burrow his way to freedom.

The Abbé and Dantès become fast friends, and as the Abbé teaches Dantès languages, history, and science, they begin to make elaborate plans to cooperate in tunneling out of the prison. After some years, they begin their labors, carefully and secretly digging through the earth beneath the foundation of the prison. Finally, they believe that they are almost ready to escape, but the Abbé cannot continue; he collapses in a cataleptic seizure. He simply cannot go on. He urges Dantès to do so, but Dantès cannot; he refuses to desert his friend. Dantès' loyalty so impresses the Abbé that when he recovers, he tells Dantès about the hidden treasure. It actually exists, the Abbé insists, and in the fourteenth century, it belonged to the famous Spada family, for whom the Abbé worked. Since there is no family remaining, the treasure now belongs to whoever finds it. It is buried, the Abbé says, in a cave on the little island of Monte Cristo.

Dantès urges Faria to resume their plans for escape and although he is very weak, the Abbé does, but again he collapses, this time in fearful and harrowing spasms, and then lies unconscious. Dantès tries to revive him, as he did before with the Abbé's potent medicine, but this time, it is to no avail.

Panicking, Dantès scurries along the secret passageway back to his own cell and waits until he thinks that it is safe to return to the Abbé's cell. When he does so, he carefully removes a stone from the cell wall and sees the Abbé's corpse encased in a shroud. His future plans crumble; he cannot think of escape any longer. He and the Abbé have been like brothers, working long and difficult hours in order to reach freedom. Now Dantès is alone. Yet a small flicker of the possibility of escape remains in Dantès, and clutching at freedom like a drowning man, he takes the Abbé's body back along the secret corridor, lays it out on his own bed, toward the wall, replaces the stone leading to their secret passageway, and hurries back to the Abbé's cell, where he stitches himself into the Abbé's shroud. And none too soon, for the prison guards arrive and lift up Dantès' stiffened body. Ominously, one of them comments that the corpse seems unusually heavy, and for an instant, Dantès is filled with fear, but nothing more is said as they carry him out of the prison. Then Dantès hears the sound of waves breaking against the rocks of the Chateau d'If.

"What miserable weather," one of the guards remarks, and they both laugh. Dantès hears a heavy object being dropped on the ground, and then he feels the sudden pain of a heavy rope being knotted around his ankles. There is more laughter, and then Dantès is heaved far out into the depths of the fierce, icy sea – the "cemetery," Dantès realizes, of this abominable prison.

Commentary

In these chapters, we have two main concerns: first, Chapters 7 and 8 are concerned with establishing the greed and the ambition of Villefort, and second, the experiences of Edmond Dantès as a prisoner in the dungeon of the Chateau d'If. Clearly, Villefort's ambitions are largely responsible for Dantès' imprisonment, and here, we also see additional evidence that "he [Villefort] would sacrifice anything to his ambition, even his own father." Villefort's ambitions also lead him to postpone his marriage to the daughter of the Marquis de Saint-Méran – if Napoleon regains power; if that happens, he will marry someone whom his father would know since his father is one of the most prominent Bonapartists in Paris; otherwise, Villefort will marry the royalist Saint-Méran's daughter – if Napoleon is again exiled. Villefort's ambition caused him to imprison Dantès, and later, because of Dantès' sense of "justice," his ambition will be his downfall.

During the early years of Dantès' imprisonment, Dantès suffers almost every stage of human emotion that can be imagined. He begins his term of imprisonment with pride and hope, being fully conscious of his innocence, but then his pride and hope are replaced by *doubt,* which is followed by fervent prayers to God. Then his soul becomes dark, and his despondency turns into wrath. In utter despair, Dantès finally decides upon suicide by starvation.

The greatness of a novel is often related to the universal appeal of that novel. For example, Dumas creates very vividly here the idea of a trapped animal which wishes desperately to escape, and we, the readers, respond completely to Dantès' desperate plight and his determination to escape because it is a basic aspect of human nature to sympathize with a trapped animal, whether it is a dog tied on a leash or a human being chained to a chain gang. Correlated with this universal idea is another scene that is now famous to almost everyone in the Western world—that is, in imprisoned solitude, one hears the faint beginnings of contact with another person.

After six years of virtual isolation in prison, Dantès finally hears an unusual and curious noise, the constant and continual scraping sounds of a prisoner trying to escape. The ray of hope that escape is possible restores Dantès to life. This scene, of course, is famous because it, or variations of it, have been the plot of many later books and untold movies about the attempted escape of innocent prisoners. Every detail of this scene has been so often repeated that it is difficult to conceive that this is the original version of the story. One can only be stunned at Dantès' realizing the *possibility* of human contact after being isolated for a full *six years.*

His contact with the Abbé Faria will be the most important contact that Dantès will ever make. For eight years, he will be a constant companion with a man who possesses one of the finest minds of that time; this is an immense stroke of good fortune for Dantès, who is himself a quick student with many natural endowments, a prodigious memory, a keen intellect, a mathematical turn of mind, the poetic strain which is in every sailor, and the ability to quickly master languages. Within a year, in addition to the French, Greek, and Italian which Dantès already knows, he adds Spanish, English, and German. Also, Dantès quickly learns history, sciences, and basic human psychology, all of which will serve him perfectly in times to come. For example, Dantès observes the psychological and analytical mind of the Abbé when, by simply questioning Dantès, the Abbé is able to identify the persons of Danglars, Caderousse, and Fernand as the people who betrayed Dantès; the Abbé is also able to determine the relationship between Villefort and Monsieur Noirtier, Villefort's father, fully explaining the motivations which prompted Villefort to have Dantès imprisoned.

The purpose of the plan to escape and the completion of the plan come at a time when both men *could* have escaped except that the Abbé has one of his rare cataleptic seizures. His life is saved by some miraculous drops which he has, but he is so weakened that he is no longer able to carry through with his plans for escape. Thus, he sends Dantès on to escape by himself, but Dantès refuses. The point of this narration is to test Dantès' loyalty – that is, the loyalty of the hero. Dantès' refusal to escape, his refusal to desert his beloved friend (or father figure) shows him to be a person essentially noble of heart and worthy of the secret which the Abbé will now share with him. In works of Romantic fiction, the hero is tried and tested and must be proven to be true and dependable. Dantès easily passes these tests; had he not been found to be true and loyal and noble, he would have escaped empty-handed, but now that he has proven himself to be noble-hearted and devoted, the Abbé will reveal the secret of the hidden treasure to him.

In a realistic novel or in real life, such virtue is not necessarily rewarded. However, in a Romantic novel, virtue is always rewarded and vice is always punished. Consequently, once Edmond Dantès has proved himself to be loyal, faithful, and trustworthy to the Abbé, he is given the history of the Spada family and the secret of the immense treasure which is hidden on the island of Monte Cristo. (One should note that the method which Abbé Faria used to discover the treasure – that is, a document written in invisible ink which becomes legible under heat – is a literary device that has now become commonplace since this novel was published.)

With the possibility of an immense fortune coming to him, Dantès thinks of "all the good a man could do for his friends with such a fortune, and at those moments, [his] face would darken because he remembered the oath of vengeance he had sworn, and he thought of how much harm a man could do to his enemies in modern times with such a fortune." When Dantès escapes, he will use his immense fortune for both purposes – to reward his friends, and to punish his enemies.

Dantès' escape from the Chateau d'If is perhaps the most daring and the most famous escape scene in all of literature. The imagination,

32

the fortitude, and the ingenuity of the escape is equalled only by the courage and desperation that it would take to exchange places with a dead man, concealing oneself in a heavy canvas bag, not knowing if you were going to be buried alive, burned, or otherwise done away with. Few people could be so desperate that they would be willing to face such unknown terrors without resorting to utter panic. Dantès' calmness in the face of such terror and adversity is the very stuff of which Romantic heroes are made. And the difficulty of the escape is correlated with the pleasure that the reader has when that escape has been effected.

Dantès' fourteen years of imprisonment represent a major portion of his life. Now thirty-three, the age at which Christ rose from the dead, Dantès escapes from prison, and he figuratively "rises from the dead" as he cuts through the burial shrouds and emerges naked into a new world as a reborn man.

Chapters 13 – 19

MONTE CRISTO'S GENEROSITY

Summary

Stunned and almost suffocating, Dantès manages to rip open the shroud-sack with a knife, and then he cuts himself free from the cannon ball that is tied around his feet. But he is still not safe. The waves around him churn and rise like phantoms. Finally, however, Dantès is able to reach the small island of Tiboulen, where, exhausted, he falls asleep on its jagged, rocky shoreline. Briefly, he wakes long enough to see a small fishing boat smashed against the rocks, its crew lost. Then, in almost disbelief, he sees a single-masted Genoese ship approaching, and snatching up a cap from one of the drowned crew of the fishing ship, he hails the tartan and is taken aboard. He tells the captain that he is Maltese, and he explains that he has a six-inch beard and foot-long hair because of a vow that he made to Our Lady of Piedigrotta. He is given trousers and a shirt and is hired on as a sailor.

Fourteen years have passed since Dantès entered prison as a handsome young stripling of nineteen. He is now thirty-three. What has happened to his beloved Mercédès in these fourteen years? And what has happened to his father? to Danglars? Fernand and Villefort? His dark eyes flash with hatred at the thought of these last three names. His spirits brighten, though, when he suddenly sees an island appear amidst the soft pink rays of the rising sun. It is the Isle of Monte Cristo, the isle of his immense, secret fortune.

Two and a half months pass, and Dantès becomes a skillful smuggler (for the boat which rescued him was a smuggler's ship). His strategy is to remain a smuggler long enough so that he can avoid all suspicion when he finally decides to sail for Monte Cristo and claim his hidden fortune. Fate lends a hand to Dantès when the captain of the smuggling ship decides to dock at Monte Cristo and make an illegal exchange of goods with a ship from the Levant.

On the island, Dantès pretends to be hunting for goats, and he does actually kill one and sends it back to camp with Jacopo, a sailor who has befriended him. Then, in order to be able to remain on the island, Dantès pretends to have hurt his leg. Reluctantly, his comrades leave him, but as soon as their ship is at sea, Dantès searches for the treasure and, with difficulty, he finally finds it in a second cavern beyond the cave which he first entered. The cask which he unearths is filled with gold coins, unpolished golden ingots, and diamonds, pearls, emeralds, and rubies. Dantès is giddy and wild. He feels on the brink of madness. All of these incalculable, fabulous riches are for him and him alone!

Six days later, the smuggling ship returns, and Dantès boards it, carrying several carefully concealed diamonds. In port, he exchanges them for a small yacht, sails for Monte Cristo, and places his immense fortune in an especially built, secret compartment on board the yacht. Then he boldly sails into the port of Marseilles with an English passport.

The narrative now moves to the south of France, to an inn that is owned by Dantès' old neighbor, Caderousse. Caderousse is visited by Dantès, disguised now as Abbé Busoni, an inquisitive priest who says that he is the executor of Dantès' will; accordingly, he asks Caderousse numerous questions about what happened to Dantès' three "friends" – Caderousse, Danglars, and Fernand – and also about the fate of Mercédès, Dantès' former fiancée. Caderousse is cautioned by his wife not to be so candid, but Caderousse loves to talk; besides, he has become very cynical about life. Thus, not knowing that it is Dantès to whom he is speaking, he reveals that:

(1) Monsieur Morrel risked his life trying to legally set the "rabid Bonapartist" (Dantès) free.

(2) Dantès' father is dead, so he has no use for Dantès' money.

(3) Danglars was no friend to Dantès; in fact, he instigated Dantès' arrest; *he* doesn't deserve Dantès' money.

(4) Fernand has been friendly with Danglars ever since he mailed Danglars' denunciation of Dantès; furthermore, he himself compromised all nationalistic and moralistic principles in order to have himself made a Count; he now lives in Paris with his wife, the beautiful Mercédès.

(5) Villefort married well, has received many honors, and is wealthy.

The "priest" (Dantès) tells Caderousse that "God's justice" demands that Caderousse be given a fabulous diamond, worth fifty thousand francs. In exchange, the "priest" asks for the "red silk purse" that Morrel, the shipowner, left full of money on Dantès' father's mantle, a purse that is now in Caderousse's possession. The "priest" then takes the purse and leaves, and Caderousse and his wife are dumbfounded at their sudden, miraculous good fortune.

Next day, Dantès, again in disguise, this time as an English gentleman, acts as a representative from the firm of Thomson and French and makes inquiries about the firm of Morrel and Son. He is told that they are rumored to be on the brink of bankruptcy. Therefore, Dantès purchases a very large account, which Morrel will soon have to pay off. Still in disguise, Dantès visits Morrel; during the visit, Morrel is told that his only remaining ship, the *Pharaon,* has sunk in a hurricane. The few half-naked sailors in Morrel's office are paid their wages and are discharged. Morrel can do no more. He has no money. But at that moment, the disguised Dantès tells Morrel that the bill which will soon be due does not have to be repaid until three months later. Morrel is so choked with emotion that he can barely speak. Before leaving, Dantès tells Julie, Morrel's daughter, that sometime in the future she will receive a message from "Sinbad the Sailor," and that she must do exactly as "Sinbad" tells her to do—"no matter how strange."

Because of the generous financial postponement offered him, Morrel is able to remain financially solvent—but only barely so. Therefore, he goes to Marseilles to ask the millionaire Danglars to guarantee a loan for him. Danglars refuses, and Morrel returns to Marseilles, overcome with humiliation and despair.

Morrel tells his family that this time, they're "lost," and Morrel fully intends to commit suicide; he tells his son, Maximilien, that if he were to live without paying his bills, he would be disgraced. If he kills himself, however, he will die – and be remembered – as "an unfortunate but honorable man." His son reluctantly understands and allows his father to be alone.

At the very moment that Morrel lifts a pistol to his mouth, his daughter cries out that they are saved! She says that she went to a house in the Allées de Meilhan, which the note from "Sinbad" asked her to do, and there she found an old red silk purse; inside it was a bill for two hundred and eighty-seven thousand, five hundred francs, marked *paid!* There was also a "diamond the size of a walnut" in the purse, alongside a small piece of parchment, which read "Julie's dowry." Then, suddenly, Julie and her father hear a voice crying out that the *Pharaon* is coming into port. Morrel's strength fails him, but the news is absolutely true: an exact duplicate of the lost *Pharaon*, with a full cargo, is ready to dock.

Unnoticed, a handsome and smiling gentleman calls out to Jacopo to bring a boat; then the two men row toward a beautifully rigged yacht. On board, the handsome gentleman looks out to sea and bids a formal farewell to "kindness, humanity and gratitude." Henceforth, he will be an agent of vengeance and will "punish the wicked." He gives a signal, and the yacht puts out to sea.

Commentary

Even the most elemental reader will recognize the Romantic technique of having the hero escape during a storm – the cliche, of course, is that the storm outside is correlated with the storm raging in the breast of the hero. Here too, the noise of the storm ironically masks Edmond Dantès' cry for freedom, and it is also ironic that Dantès is rescued by smugglers and that the young smuggler Jacopo will ultimately become the captain of the yacht of the Count of Monte Cristo, another indication that the Count is always generous with those who have been kind to him.

Edmond Dantès has been in prison for fourteen years, and during that time he has not shaved nor had a haircut, yet he is able to successfully account for these matters by his ingenious story that he made a religious vow not to cut his hair for ten years.

When Dantès does cut his hair, he is drastically changed. He entered the Chateau d'If with the round and smiling face of a happy young man. Now his oval face has lengthened, his lips have taken on a line of firm resolution, and his eyebrows now possess a thoughtful wrinkle; his eyes are of deep sadness with occasional flashes of dark hatred, and his skin has grown wan and pale. Thus, Dantès' physical attributes have changed to the point that his old enemies will not recognize him, and, consequently, he will be able to move among them with complete anonymity, effecting his revenge without suspicion. (As we later discover, only Mercédès, the woman he was about to marry when he was arrested, recognizes him, and she does not reveal his secret.)

More important, Edmond Dantès has changed inwardly. Because of the tutelage of Abbé Faria, he has mastered many languages, he has learned much history and politics, he has studied mathematics and the sciences, and he has been exposed to treachery and betrayal by honorable men in high places. Thus, the deep learning that Dantès has acquired is now reflected in his face by an expression of intelligent self-confidence. Certainly, he is no longer the trusting and naive young man that he was at the beginning of his imprisonment fourteen years ago.

In Chapter 15, we have the search for buried treasure. Here, Dumas appeals to a very basic instinct in human nature by having Edmond Dantès discover a secret treasure of untold value – diamonds, rubies, emeralds, pearls, and gold coins of immense value are now in his possession. The universality invoked is that most people have, at some time or other in their lives, harbored a dream of discovering a buried treasure, or else they have dreamed that they might, in some way, become the sudden recipient of untold wealth. This human desire can be found in works from Homer's *Iliad* (when the hero Achilles is offered all sorts of valuable prizes if he will return to war) to Stevenson's *Treasure Island,* and to modern-day TV shows, which give away large sums of money. The search for buried treasure is one of the many universals that Dumas uses to involve his reader in his exciting adventure story.

In order to stay on the island of Monte Cristo, Dantès has to create an ingenious ruse to persuade the smugglers to leave him there. But

Dantès' plan *almost* fails because Jacopo wants to stay with him—even though that would mean that Jacopo would sacrifice his rather significant share in the smuggling profits. Thus, this particularly unselfish act is a correlation to Dantès' resolve to remain with the ailing Abbé Faria, and in a lesser way, Jacopo will also be rewarded for his unselfishness and for his devotion to Dantès; he will become the trusted servant and friend that Edmond Dantès needs so badly at this time in his life.

In Chapters 15 and 16, Dantès discovers what has transpired during his imprisonment. Then he goes to his old neighbor, Gaspard Caderousse, and all of the projections of Abbé Faria about Dantès' "friends" are confirmed by Caderousse—that is, Danglars wrote the letter of betrayal, and it was mailed by Fernand—both of whom are now wealthy and titled men of France. In addition, Dantès learns of all the wrongs which were perpetrated against him, and of the people like Monsieur Morrel who risked his own life trying to obtain Dantès' release.

This section illustrates particularly well how thoroughly Dantès has learned the basic psychology of mankind during his tutorials with Abbé Faria; that is, in his disguise as Abbé Busoni, Dantès shows a diamond worth fifty thousand francs to Caderousse, suggesting that the diamond is to be divided between Dantès' four old friends and Dantès' father. Dantès, however, is absolutely certain that Caderousse, because of greed, will tell the exact (and damning) truth about Danglars, Fernand, and Villefort. Dantès' father is dead and is of no matter to Caderousse. And, as is apparent to both the reader and to Dantès, Caderousse convicts himself of the most base treachery in his narration so as to get full and sole possession of the diamond; ultimately, he will murder a jeweler from Paris, as well as his own wife, and thereby enter upon a career of all sorts of crime until he is finally apprehended by Abbé Busoni (alias the Count of Monte Cristo).

Chapter 17 serves a double purpose. By buying financial notes (two hundred thousand francs worth) which would aid his old friend and benefactor (Monsieur Morrel) from the Director of Prisons, Monsieur de Boville, Dantès is able to gain access to all the prison records and thus confirm whose handwriting assigned him to supposedly life imprisonment; the handwriting is Villefort's.

During Caderousse's narration, it is furthermore discovered that *all* of Dantès' enemies have prospered and are now among the most powerful and the most wealthy men of France. It would have been an easy or simple task of revenge if all of his enemies had remained simple and unpretentious people. Instead, all except Caderousse have prospered tremendously, and thus, Dantès' task of revenge will be more involved. That is, their wealth, their political influence, and their power make the Count's task of revenge much more complicated and difficult, but also, to use the common cliche, "the bigger they are, the harder they fall." Dantès, of course, will finally be able to topple the most powerful, the most wealthy, and the most influential men of France by using slow and deliberate subterfuges. If readers are ever tempted to sympathize with the victims, they should always keep foremost in mind how Edmond Dantès suffered in prison for *fourteen* long and miserable years as the result of their treachery.

At the end of Chapter 19, Dantès has now used his wealth to perform all sorts of good deeds – to reinstate Monsieur Morrel and to re-establish the Morrel family name. The rest of the novel will show how Dantès (now about to assume the identity of the Count of Monte Cristo) effects his revenge upon his enemies. As Dantès himself expresses it: "And now farewell to kindness, humanity, and gratitude. Farewell to all sentiments that gladden the heart. I have substituted myself for Providence in rewarding the good. May the God of Vengeance now yield me His place to punish the wicked!"

Chapters 20–21

MONTE CRISTO'S REVENGE

Summary

The scene now changes dramatically. We are in Rome, where two new characters appear: Franz d'Epinay (a young baron) and Albert de Morcerf (a good-looking viscount). The young men are fretting because they have come to Rome to find romance and laughter during the carnival season, but strangely, all of Rome's carriages and horses have been rented. The two young men are furious; men of their class do *not* "run around Rome on foot like lawyers' clerks." Nevertheless, they decide to deliver their "letters of introduction" to all of Rome's first families and make plans, if need be, to costume themselves as colorful "Neapolitan harvesters" and ride around in a festive and be-ribboned oxcart. But at the last minute, the two men are saved by a stroke of good fortune: the hotel-keeper tells them that the "very great" Count of Monte Cristo has heard of their plight and has offered them two seats in *his* carriage, as well as two seats in *his* window above the square where most of the merriment will take place.

When Franz and Albert meet Monte Cristo, they are in awe of him and of his palatial quarters and his princely generosity. In addition, both men are startled by Monte Cristo's enthusiastic invitation to join him in witnessing a public execution from a window overlooking the execution site. Both Albert and Franz survive the ordeal, but they are both greatly distraught. Immediately before the execution, Monte Cristo talks of little else except the justice of slow and painful revenge; the guillotine, he feels, offers death too quickly and too painlessly. In contrast to instantaneous decapitation, however, Franz and Albert witness a singularly savage execution: a man is bludgeoned with a mace, his throat slit open, and his stomach trampled on until jets of blood spurt from his mouth like fantastic ruby-colored fountains. Curiously, the other prisoner on the block, a bronzed and handsome young man with a wild, proud look in his eyes, is pardoned at the last minute – as Monte Cristo prophecied earlier that he would be.

Hurriedly, the two men and Monte Cristo don their carnival costumes and join the festivities. Albert is soon rewarded with romance; a masked lady in a carriage tosses a bouquet of violets to him, and on the second day of the carnival, she tosses another bouquet to him; then Albert is rewarded with an invitation to a rendezvous with the mysterious lady. He goes to the appointed street, but at the moment when all of the carnival candles are suddenly extinguished in a dramatic finale, he is kidnapped.

Franz receives a note demanding a great deal of money and threatening Albert's life if the sum is not paid. In desperation, Franz asks Monte Cristo for a loan, explaining that a man waits below for the ransom money. Monte Cristo goes to the window and speaks to the fellow. It is Peppino, the handsome, tanned youth who was pardoned earlier, and who, it turns out, "owes his life" to Monte Cristo. He explains that his master, the notorious Luigi Vampa, kidnapped Albert. Monte Cristo immediately tells Peppino to take them to Vampa at once.

Deep in the bowels of Rome's catacombs, Monte Cristo accuses Vampa of breaking his vow *never* to molest a friend of the Count's. Vampa, more like a gallant gentleman than a bandit, profusely apologizes to Monte Cristo and immediately releases Albert. Later, Albert asks Monte Cristo how he can ever repay him for saving his life, and Monte Cristo answers that he would like to be introduced into Parisian society. Albert, of course, promises to do so, and he sets a date for their next meeting – in Paris, in exactly three months. The two men shake hands on the agreement, and Monte Cristo leaves. Franz turns to Albert and says that Monte Cristo is indeed a strange man; he feels uneasy about the Count's coming to Paris.

Commentary

These two transitional chapters show Edmond Dantès now totally metamorphosed into the noble, distinguished, and very rich Count of Monte Cristo. Quite a number of years have passed since the episode with Monsieur Morrel, and we can only gather from later facts that the Count has traveled extensively and performed many acts – such as acquiring Ali, his mute valet, Bertuccio, his steward, and Haydée, his "slave-mistress." And note that although it seems that the Count is "accidentally" staying in the same hotel with Albert de Morcerf and Franz d'Epinay, and although it seems to be a "miraculous" rescue of Albert, there is every indication (virtual proof, in fact) that Monte Cristo has arranged these things to happen so that he can "seemingly" come to the rescue of these two young (and prestigious) Parisian gentlemen. In other words, the Count of Monte Cristo wants Albert to become so indebted to him that Albert will introduce him into Paris society, and thereby introduce him to the very enemies against whom he plans his revenge. The first and simplest obligation which Albert owes to Monte Cristo is, of course, the loan of a carriage when one was "suddenly impossible to obtain" during Rome's carnival season. But the major obligation occurs when Monte Cristo "saved Albert's life" after he was "captured" by the bandit Luigi Vampa, a person who is also obligated to the Count. Albert is obligated to such an extent, therefore, that he will gladly introduce Monte Cristo to prominent Parisian society, where Monte Cristo will begin his slow revenge against those who are responsible for his long years of brutal imprisonment.

In this section also, we discover Monte Cristo's philosophy of revenge and death. Since the Count could obviously hire an assassin, or in other ways bring about the *immediate* death of his enemies, we should note that he does *not* believe in a quick and easy death for a person who has made others suffer for a long and extended period of time. As he says, "If a man has tortured and killed your father, your mother, your sweetheart, one of those beings who leave an eternal emptiness and a perpetually bleeding wound when they are torn from your heart . . . do you think society has given you sufficient reparation because the man who made you undergo long years of mental and emotional suffering has undergone a few seconds of physical pain?" In other words, Monte Cristo does *not* want quick revenge—he wants *slow* and *deliberate* vengeance: "For slow, profound, infinite, and eternal suffering, I'd try to avenge myself by inflicting similar suffering—an eye for an eye, and a tooth for a tooth." Thus, Monte Cristo will bring revenge upon his enemies slowly and very deliberately, making those who made him suffer, suffer in turn, for a very long time.

Chapters 22 – 26

CADEROUSSE'S VILLAINY

Summary

In Paris, three months later, Albert impatiently awaits the arrival of Monte Cristo for a luncheon party. The first guest to arrive is Lucien Debray, the tall, blond Secretary to the Minister of the Interior (we discover later that he is Danglars' wife's lover). Among the other guests is Captain Maximilien Morrel, a tall, dark, and broad-chested young man who is the only son of Monsieur Morrel, the owner of the lost *Pharaon*, which Monte Cristo financially "resurrected" and thereby saved Morrel's shipping firm. Young Morrel, it is revealed, once saved a nobleman's life in Constantinople, and because Morrel's father's life was once "miraculously" saved, Maximilien tries to do "some heroic action" every year.

Albert then tells his guests about his own "miraculous" rescue by the Count of Monte Cristo. One of the guests says that no such "Count" exists; he knows *all* of Europe's nobility, and he has *never* heard of the

Count *nor* of the island of Monte Cristo. But, at the very stroke of ten-thirty, Monte Cristo is announced.

Over lunch, Monte Cristo impresses them all with his pillbox, fashioned out of a magnificent, hollowed-out emerald; then he tells them of his daring adventures with Luigi Vampa, the bandit king, and mentions that his steward, Bertuccio, was once a bandit and that he, Monte Cristo, was influential enough to save the life of the handsome Peppino, Vampa's bandit-liaison. In turn, Albert tells Monte Cristo about his fiancée, Eugénie Danglars (the daughter of the purser on the *Pharaon*, that Dantès was once to have commanded). The young men enjoy the story and are so impressed by Albert's guest that they plead to be allowed to help Monte Cristo secure a lodging, but the Count tells them that he already has a Paris address – 30 Champs Elysées (Paris' most famous boulevard). They are all stunned at such costly originality, and thus, they beg to introduce him to a Parisian mistress of their choice. But Monte Cristo says that he has already chosen a mistress; she is his "slave," whom he bought in Constantinople, and who speaks nothing but modern Greek. Clearly, Monte Cristo is one of the most extraordinary men whom any of the young Parisian noblemen have ever known.

After the others have gone, Albert shows Monte Cristo around his apartment, pointing out an oil portrait of his mother dressed as a Catalan fisherwoman. Monte Cristo admires the portrait (it is a stunning likeness of the beautiful and beloved Mercédès, who is, we will learn, Albert's mother; Albert's father is Fernand, who "bought" his title of Count de Morcerf as soon as he was rich enough to afford it). Later, in the salon of Albert's parents, Monte Cristo meets Mercédès and his old rival, Fernand. Fernand apparently does not recognize the immensely wealthy and distinguished Monte Cristo, whom he knew years ago as Edmond Dantès (we discover later that Mercédès recognized Dantès immediately). Both of the Morcerfs are deeply grateful to Monte Cristo for saving Albert's life, but Mercédès is obviously stunned when she first sees Monte Cristo. She explains her unusual behavior as only that of any mother who suddenly meets the man who has saved her son's life. Monte Cristo, however, is even paler than Mercédès, and he soon excuses himself, explaining that he has yet to see his new house in Paris. After he leaves, Mercédès questions her son: does Monte Cristo like Albert? Is Albert fond of Monte Cristo? Albert defends Monte Cristo with great fervor, not noticing that his mother is deeply absorbed in her own thoughts, her eyes closed.

When Monte Cristo returns to his city residence, he prepares to sign the necessary papers to buy his "country house," and we discover that instead of its being outside of Paris, it is *in* Paris, in the suburb of Auteuil, opposite the Bois de Boulogne, an enormous park within the city environs of Paris. (This house will be the scene of one of Monte Cristo's most startling "revelations.")

Bertuccio, Monte Cristo's steward, is clearly but unexplainably upset when he hears the word "Auteuil"; later, he crosses himself fearfully when he learns that he will have to live in the house with Monte Cristo. The Count questions Bertuccio about his unnatural fear of the country house, and we learn that:

(1) The house formerly belonged to Saint-Méran, the father of the woman who was Villefort's first wife. She died, but Villefort continued to make mysterious visits to this house, where he kept a young lady. Bertuccio went to the house, hoping to murder Villefort, the public prosecutor, because Villefort refused to find the murderer of Bertuccio's brother.

(2) At the house, Bertuccio saw Villefort come out with a spade and bury a small box. Bertuccio stabbed Villefort and uncovered the box. Thinking that it might contain money, he found, instead, a newborn baby boy. He took the child to his sister-in-law, and he remembers that the baby's swaddling clothes were marked with a crown and the initials *H* and *N*.

(3) The years passed, and when the boy was eleven, Bertuccio feared that he was becoming irredeemably perverse. Then one night, Bertuccio was almost arrested by customs officers, but was able to escape and flee to an inn run by a clever scoundrel, Caderousse. Bertuccio spied Caderousse bargaining with a jeweler, trying to get as much money as possible for a magnificent diamond that Caderousse and his wife swore was a gift from a sailor named Edmond Dantès.

(4) The jeweler finally gave Caderousse forty-five thousand francs and hurried away amidst a violent thunderstorm. He returned, soaked to the skin, and asked for a bed. The Caderousses fed him, and later in the night, Bertuccio heard a pistol shot and a terrible shriek. He got up and saw Caderousse covered with blood and clutching the diamond; he disappeared into the darkness. Upstairs, Bertuccio found the corpse of Madame Caderousse, as well as that of the jeweler, a

kitchen knife plunged in his chest. Immediately, Bertuccio was arrested by the customs officers who followed him.

(5) Five days before Bertuccio's trial, Abbé Busoni came to prison and vouched for the truth of Bertuccio's story about the diamond. Meanwhile, Caderousse was arrested, confessed everything, and was sentenced to hard labor for life. Bertuccio was released and sought out Monte Cristo, as the Abbé told him to do. He has been Monte Cristo's trusted steward ever since.

Bertuccio's story finally finished, Monte Cristo and his steward return to Paris.

Dantès' plans for revenge have begun. He has spun a web of deception and has already caught Fernand, his old rival for Mercédès, and, in addition, he has found Mercédès, and he has ferreted out Danglars, as well as Monsieur Morrel's son, Maximilien – and he has also cornered Villefort, who did *not* die when Bertuccio stabbed him. (Villefort, remember, named Dantès as a traitor to the state and signed Dantès' indictment; Danglars wrote the initial letter condemning Dantès, and Fernand mailed the letter. Because of these men, Dantès almost died during his fourteen years in prison.) Now, Dantès (as the awesome Monte Cristo) will create more "coincidences" so that he can ingratiate himself to certain other people and make them *all* feel "deeply obligated" to him.

First, Monte Cristo begins his revenge on Danglars and his wife. Danglars presents his wife with two handsome, dappled grey horses which are supposedly the finest horses in Paris. Monte Cristo sees the horses, admires them, and orders his steward to buy them. Bertuccio obeys, and then Monte Cristo goes to visit Danglars, where the two men discuss finances. Monte Cristo convinces him to open a checking account for him so that he can draw instant cash up to six million francs. Danglars finally agrees, although reluctantly, with a pale and nervous smile. Monte Cristo then meets Danglars' wife and discovers that she is being entertained by young Debray, whom Monte Cristo met earlier at Albert's luncheon. Debray glances out the window and sees Madame Danglars' prize horses harnessed to Monte Cristo's carriage. Madame Danglars is furious with her husband for selling the horses, and Monte Cristo feigns ignorance of the whole affair. Later, Monte Cristo sends a note of profuse apology to Madame Danglars and returns her horses with a gift of large, awesome, flashing diamonds in each of their silver rosettes.

Next, Villefort's wife, Héloise, borrows these fabulous horses from Madame Danglars, and Monte Cristo arranges to have the horses "run away." Then, "by accident," Monte Cristo's mute Nubian servant, Ali, is able to stop the horses dramatically in front of Monte Cristo's house, and the Count is able to administer a few drops of a potent liquid (the same that Abbé Faria used in prison) to rally the faint young Villefort child, Edouard. Héloise is absolutely bewitched by Monte Cristo, and she says that she is in his debt forever because of his "goodness and generosity."

That evening, Villefort visits Monte Cristo to thank him for saving his wife and his son. The two men talk, and Monte Cristo reveals that he has made a study of all men in all countries on all continents. He knows all their virtues, all their vices, and all their weaknesses. He tells Villefort that men are, at heart, "ugly creatures." Unlike other men, however, Monte Cristo belongs to no country, nor is he identifiable as being a certain "kind" of man. He is extraordinary. He fears no one because he is able to determine immediately whether a man is sufficiently advantageous enough to be useful to him. All men, he says, have committed "either errors or crimes," and long ago, Monte Cristo set himself up as Providence, as it were, to "reward and punish." Arrogantly, Villefort remarks that while Madame de Villefort may see herself as merely the Count's "eternal friend," he – that is, Villefort – wants Monte Cristo to recognize that *he* is *"not* an ordinary man. Not at all."

Commentary

Six months later, and after many years of preparation in which the Count of Monte Cristo seems to know *every detail* about his enemies, we are now presented with his first direct meeting with his enemies, and we learn the various methods which he will use to get each one of them either obligated to him or involved with him in some financial way. Thus, we can assume again that, as he himself announced, the reason for his so-called "rescue" of Albert de Morcerf was so that he would be able to meet intimately with Albert's father, Count de Morcerf, alias Fernand Mondego, his old rival for Mercédès.

At the breakfast (brunch by today's standards) that Albert has arranged for the Count, Maximilien Morrel unexpectedly is there and, moreover, the Count learns that Maximilien's sister, Julie, has been happily married for nine years; therefore, we know that the Count would now be around forty-one or forty-two years old, and we may assume that during these intervening years, Monte Cristo has spent his time investing his money, increasing his knowledge of his enemies, and establishing his power in the world at large. It is particularly ironic that the Count is described at the breakfast party as being the "savior" of young Albert, and that Maximilien is there as the "savior" of another of the guests. This will allow the Count to become friends with Morrel and, ultimately, become his protector.

Among the young group, the Count is quite outspoken. He explains that his steward, Bertuccio, was probably once a smuggler who is now obligated to him; that his valet is a mute Nubian whose life he once saved; that his mistress is a woman he bought out of slavery; and that the people who kidnapped Albert Morcerf are people for whom he once performed acts requiring gratitude—for example, he kept Luigi Vampa from being captured by the Italian police, and it was he who saved Peppino's life during the carnival in Rome.

After the party, Albert introduces the Count to his parents, who acknowledge their deep indebtedness to him for having saved their son's life. Monte Cristo's old acquaintance Fernand (Count de Morcerf) does not recognize him, of course, but we are made aware that Mercédès does indeed recognize the Count as her fiancé of long ago, Edmond Dantès, but she will keep his secret until much later in the novel, only to reveal it to her son to keep him from dueling with the Count.

In the history that Bertuccio relates of his own life and experiences, we must remember that the Count of Monte Cristo has already heard all of these experiences; unknowingly, Bertuccio confessed them to the Count when Monte Cristo was disguised as the Abbé Busoni. Consequently, the Count has already heard Bertuccio's story and has arranged to buy the house which Bertuccio talks about. Monte Cristo wants to *test* Bertuccio's veracity and *insure* that Bertuccio will always be totally and completely loyal to him. Through Bertuccio's story, we learn of the almost total depravity of Caderousse and of the baseness of Benedetto, the son of the present Madame Danglars (the mysterious "lady" at Auteuil) and Villefort.

By the end of this section, Monte Cristo has also involved himself with Danglars—by means of letters of investment—to the tune of six million francs—and he has rescued Madame de Villefort and her son,

Edouard, from the runaway carriage which the Count caused to be a runaway carriage so that he could rescue it. Thus, he has deeply obligated the Villefort family to him.

When Villefort himself comes to express his appreciation to the Count for having saved the lives of his wife and their son, the Count is once again able to express his views concerning rewards and punishments. The Count maintains that if he were, like Christ, offered anything in the world which he could choose, he would reply: "I have always heard of Providence, yet I have never seen it or anything resembling it, which makes me think it does not exist. I want to be Providence, for the greatest, the most beautiful and the most sublime thing I know of in this world is *to reward and punish.*"

At the end of this section, then, Monte Cristo has not encountered quite all of his enemies, but he has made those whom he has encountered extremely obligated to him in one way or another, and he will continue to follow his philosophy of *slowly* avenging himself.

Chapters 27–38

THE SECRET OF BENEDETTO'S BIRTH

Summary

At home, Monte Cristo visits Haydée, his soft and beautiful slave girl; he reminds her that they are in Paris now. Therefore, she is free to dress as a Westerner, meet other people, especially other men, and fall in love if she pleases – but Haydée says that she will *never* find a more handsome man than the Count. She loves only him, and she will never, ever leave him. Minutes later, Monte Cristo alights at the residence of Monsieur Morrel's daughter, Julie, who is now Madame Emmanuel Herbault; young Maximilien Morrel, we learn, also lives here. Inside, Monte Cristo notices a red silk purse, lying on a black velvet cushion inside a hollow crystal globe, alongside a handsome diamond in another crystal globe. (This is the diamond which Monte Cristo secretly presented for Julie's dowry.)

Maximilien and his sister relate the history of their strange and wonderous good fortune; their "angel," as they call the mysterious person who is responsible for all their material magnificence, is an Englishman representing the firm of Thomson and French of Rome.

Monte Cristo half-teases them that perhaps he knows their "angel"; the mysterious man might be a certain Lord Wilmore, who is known to perform deeds of immense, anonymous generosity. His whereabouts, however, are unknown. Maximilien then says that Morrel, their father, told them that he was convinced that their secret benefactor was none other than Edmond Dantès. The Count suddenly grows deathly pale, hurriedly pays his compliments to the Herbaults, then excuses himself. Afterward, Julie remarks that she is absolutely sure that she has heard the Count's voice before.

The Count arrives at the Villefort residence ostensibly to repay Villefort's visit, but he learns that Villefort is dining with the chancellor, and so he decides to spend the time visiting with Villefort's wife, his teenage daughter Valentine, and his son Edouard. Edouard is mutilating a beautiful picture album until his mother snatches it from him, and Valentine stays only briefly, but for the few moments that Monte Cristo sees her, he is very impressed with her gracious and forthright manner.

When Monte Cristo and Madame de Villefort are alone, he reminds her that they spoke together once before; they were in Italy, and because Monte Cristo had used his knowledge of chemistry to cure a hotelkeeper of jaundice, he acquired an instant reputation as a "great doctor." Madame de Villefort questions Monte Cristo closely about medicines and poisons. She reveals to us — and to Monte Cristo — that she herself knows a great deal about poisons. And before Monte Cristo leaves, she has managed, she thinks innocently, to make him promise to send her some of his potent liquid which he used to rouse Edouard after he fainted during the "run-away accident." Monte Cristo warns Madame de Villefort that "one drop restores life . . . but five or six drops kill." The next day, she receives the potion.

Several days later, when Albert (Mercédès' son) and Debray (Madame Danglars' lover) call on Monte Cristo, they immediately notice that the Count's house on the Champs Elysées has already acquired the palatial air of Monte Cristo himself. Albert has come for a specific reason: he wants to talk to Monte Cristo about his expected engagement to Eugénie, the elder daughter of Danglars. Eugénie is, Albert confesses, "too rich for me." Such wealth, he says, frightens him. His mother (Mercédès) is also against his marrying Eugénie. But his father (Fernand) is hoping that Albert will marry Eugénie. Meanwhile, Monte Cristo seems strangely agitated; he speaks of the Danglars' fabulous wealth, and suddenly Albert suggests to Debray that since he is the minister's secretary, he could teach an invaluable lesson to the speculating-prone Madame Danglars – an especially good lesson if she is soon to be Albert's mother-in-law. Albert suggests that Debray drop a fabricated rumor about a certain political situation that will make certain stocks a wise investment; then, next day, Beauchamps, the journalist, can publish a refutation of that rumor, and the stocks would collapse, and Madame Danglars will lose a good deal of money. Several "doses of this medicine" will make the woman "more cautious." Albert (but *not* Monte Cristo) is totally oblivious to Debray's deep embarrassment. (If Debray were to do this, of course, he would be betraying his mistress and, as we will find out later, he would be creating financial disaster for himself because Madame Danglars splits her "winnings" with Debray.) Not surprisingly, Debray cuts his visit to Monte Cristo short.

Afterward, Monte Cristo proposes to Albert that perhaps he, Monte Cristo, should have a dinner party and invite the Villeforts and the Danglars – but *not* the Morcerfs. That way, Monte Cristo can spare Albert's mother (Mercédès) the pain of seeing her son with Danglars' daughter, Eugénie. "I wish to avoid that [pain to Mercédès] at all costs," Monte Cristo tells Albert. Albert, of course, is extremely grateful and says that he will tell his mother about Monte Cristo's thoughtfulness. Meanwhile, Albert will arrange matters so that it will be *impossible* for him and his family to dine with Monte Cristo – because of a "previous commitment." The Count then tells Albert that he is going to meet with a Major Cavalcanti and assist Cavalcanti's son, Andrea (in actuality, this is Villefort's and Madame Danglars' bastard son, Benedetto), to make his entrance into Parisian society. Albert jokes, yet seriously, that Monte Cristo should *also* assist Andrea to make the acquaintance of Eugénie. (Remember, however, that Eugénie is Andrea's – Benedetto's – half-sister; they share the same father, Villefort.)

That night at seven, Major Cavalcanti meets with the Count, and it is immediately clear that Cavalcanti is an imposter whom Monte Cristo is grooming for a "role," for which he is being paid an enormous sum. Monte Cristo furnishes him a birth certificate for his "son," Andrea, as well as a trunk of suitable clothing for himself. Then Monte Cristo introduces Cavalcanti to his "son," a tall blond man with flashing black eyes and a red beard. The two men agree that they must play their parts well. Monte Cristo then instructs his two "actors" to be at his house on Saturday for a dinner party. The secret web of revenge that Monte Cristo is weaving is clearly well planned, because he is preparing a series of slow and extremely painful acts of revenge upon his enemies.

We now eavesdrop on the Villefort home, where Maximilien Morrel is at a grilled iron gate. Rendezvousing with Valentine Villefort, he learns how unhappy she will be if she is forced to marry Franz d'Epinay; Maximilien vows that he will love no one else but Valentine — no matter what happens. Then, hearing voices, Valentine returns to the house where her grandfather (Monsieur Noirtier, the Bonapartist, now a paralyzed mute) is revising his will with commands from his eyes. Two notaries have been summoned. The old man's fortune, we learn, is large, almost a million francs, all of which he intends to leave to the poor — if Valentine marries Franz. Villefort (a royalist, as opposed to a Bonapartist) is furious with his father, but he knows that the old man is not *only* politically stubborn; he is stubborn by nature, and so he instructs the notaries to make the will according to Noirtier's wishes.

Leaving his father's room, Villefort learns that he and his wife have a guest: the Count of Monte Cristo, who reminds them that he expects them for dinner on Saturday at his country home in *Auteuil*. Villefort pales at that word, and even more so when Monte Cristo tells them that his "country home" once belonged to the Saint-Mérans (Villefort's former in-laws); Villefort, remember, used this house as a rendezvous site with the present Madame Danglars; in addition, Villefort believes that he buried their newborn baby alive in what is now Monte Cristo's garden. This is the house, then, where Benedetto — "Andrea Cavalcanti" — was born.

That Saturday, Monte Cristo's guests arrive — Maximilien Morrel, Lucien Debray (Madame Danglars' lover), the Danglars (the Baron, looking extremely pale and dreamy; he speaks to a cactus, and it pricks him), the "Cavalcantis" (father and son, resplendent in new finery), and the Villeforts (Monsieur Villefort is "visibly agitated").

Privately, Bertuccio (Monte Cristo's steward) excitedly tells his master that Madame Danglars is the pregnant woman whom he saw having a rendezvous with Villefort — the man whom Bertuccio was positive that he killed! The Count explains to his steward that Bertuccio's knife lodged between the wrong ribs. Then Bertuccio spies young Cavalcanti – and realizes that the young man is Benedetto, the child who was such a menace to Bertuccio's late sister-in-law!

Bertuccio staggers back to the dining room, scarcely believing his eyes, but he is able to serve dinner. And over the many opulent and exotic dishes, Monte Cristo tells his guests of the strange history of the house. Villefort begins drinking rapidly, particularly when Monte Cristo asks them all to view a "peculiar bedroom," where one's imagination might conjure up a dark night when someone might carry away "some sinister burden." At these words, Madame Danglars half-faints and asks for no more stories. Monte Cristo suggests, instead, that perhaps this room could just as well have been a bedroom for a wondrous birth! At this, Madame Danglars groans and faints. (Remember that she gave birth to Benedetto – that is, Andrea Cavalcanti – in this room and that Villefort stole away to bury the infant alive.) Villefort cries out that Madame Danglars is ill and should be taken to her carriage.

Instead, Monte Cristo takes her to another bedroom, administers a drop of his potent red liquid, and she regains consciousness. Then Monte Cristo tells them all that a crime was indeed committed in this house and that one of his workmen unearthed a wooden box containing the skeleton of a newborn baby. Madame Danglars and Villefort both tremble visibly. Cavalcanti remarks that in *his* country, the criminals would have had their heads cut off. Villefort makes a comment, but only barely, in a voice "scarcely human." Then Monte Cristo reminds his guests that they must return to their coffee. Villefort whispers to Madame Danglars that she must meet him tomorrow at his office.

Shortly afterward, the guests begin to depart. And as Andrea Cavalcanti is about to climb into his carriage, he is stopped by a bearded, ragged man with glittering eyes and teeth as sharp and white as a wolf's – it is Caderousse, and he addresses Andrea by his real name, Benedetto. Andrea quickly ushers Caderousse into his cab and tells the driver that the two men need to talk in private. Then, as Andrea drives away, Caderousse reminds him that he used to share his soup and beans with Andrea in prison; now he expects the same from Andrea, *or Benedetto!* Moreover, he needs money *now,* and so Andrea gives it to him, of course, but he touches his pistol meanwhile. And Caderousse, in turn, fingers his long Spanish knife. It is a stand-off, and so Andrea agrees to take Caderousse into Paris. When they are on the outskirts of the inner city, Caderousse snatches Andrea's hat, grabs his groom's overcoat, and leaps out of the cab, vanishing down a side street.

When the Danglars arrive home, young Debray tries to comfort Madame Danglars, but Monsieur Danglars abruptly sends him home so that he can rail at his wife in private because of her speculation debts – which have *also* cost Danglars a small fortune. He knows that Madame Danglars gambles with her "allowance" and then splits the profits with Debray. Now Danglars wants *Debray* to pay him the exact amount that Danglars has lost. Danglars names Debray outright as his wife's lover, and he accuses his wife of taking some very bad financial advice from Debray. But it was advice which Danglars followed also. He announces to his wife that he knows about *all* of her lovers – from Villefort to Debray – and he has never complained before, but heretofore, none of them cost him money. Now, Debray has caused him to lose an enormous amount of money; he will no longer be silent, and Debray must pay up. If Debray goes bankrupt, then he can leave Paris – as all bankrupts do. Danglars leaves then, and his wife collapses, in *utter* disbelief of all of the disasters that have suddenly enveloped her.

Next day, Danglars notes that young Debray's carriage does *not* arrive when it usually does, and that "by coincidence," his wife leaves in her carriage. Mid-afternoon, Danglars drives to Monte Cristo's residence on the Champs Elysées. He tells the Count about a series of financial disasters that have befallen him, and then he asks what he should do about a new problem – Cavalcanti's request for credit. The Count changes the subject. He suggests that young Andrea Cavalcanti has been brought to Paris to find a wife to share his immense fortune. Danglars intimates that he would be willing to speculate with his daughter's (Eugénie's) future if she weren't "unofficially" engaged to Albert (Mercédès' son). Monte Cristo then asks about Albert's father's past (Fernand's past, that is), and Danglars recalls a dark, mysterious "secret" concerning the "Ali Pasha affair." Monte Cristo urges Danglars to solve this mystery – especially if this man might someday be Eugénie's father-in-law, and Danglars agrees to do so – and to tell Monte Cristo if he learns, perchance, "some scandalous piece of news."

Commentary

The middle portion of the novel deals with many diverse matters. Mainly, we are concerned with the Count's involving his enemies in one way or another with their eventual downfall. The first two chapters deal with the Count's relationship with his "slave," Haydée, and his deep, fatherly affection for her and her deep devotion to him as a man. Likewise, Monte Cristo pays a visit to the grown children of Monsieur Morrel, the shipowner, the Count's first benefactor. At Julie's house, where Maximilien lives, Monte Cristo hears that both Julie and Maximilien long to discover the name of their family's secret benefactor and that their father died believing that their benefactor was Edmond Dantès.

Monte Cristo then visits the Villefort residence, and he is received as the "savior" of Villefort's wife and son. Monte Cristo reminds Madame de Villefort that they once met in Perugia (Italy), when the Count was healing a servant and a hotelkeeper, and he reveals his knowledge of medicinal herbs, especially poisonous ones. And while the Count is explaining how one drop of his liquid brought her son back to life, but that a few more drops would have killed him, Madame de Villefort's curiosity is aroused out of all proportion to the discussion; she wants some of Monte Cristo's "medicine" (poison) for her own use. At the end of their conversation, the Count acknowledges that he's convinced that "the seed I have sown has not fallen on barren ground." This is a part of his plan for slow revenge. Significantly, Madame de Villefort will prove to be the ultimate villainess of this novel; she will deliberately poison three people and will attempt to poison even her own stepdaughter.

The Count's revenge becomes more complicated when he includes Benedetto in his scheme. Benedetto is the illegitimate son of Villefort and Madame Danglars, and Monte Cristo is paying Benedetto to pretend to be the extremely wealthy son of an Italian nobleman because ultimately, the Count will intrigue Baron Danglars into arranging a marriage between Benedetto (alias Andrea Cavalcanti) and Danglars' daughter, who is (unbeknownst to Andrea) Benedetto's half-sister. Throughout this novel, we must always remember that the Count wants his revenge to be slow and *deliberate*; an immediate or quick revenge would not do justice to the suffering which he himself has undergone.

We also learn that Maximilien Morrel, the son of the Count's first employer, and Valentine de Villefort, the daughter of the Count's worst enemy, are in love with each other. And furthermore, we discover that while Maximilien feels that the Count is especially favorable in his cause, Valentine, on the contrary, feels a dislike for the Count because she senses that he has completely ignored her and her plans in order to use her in some way. (This is not found in some of the abridged editions.) Both feelings are indeed true. The Count will take no interest in Valentine until he discovers that Maximilien is deeply in love with her, and then he will leave no stone uncovered to help her.

Monsieur Noirtier is introduced in these chapters. We first heard of him when Edmond Dantès was supposed to deliver a letter to him (allegedly from Napoleon) and was arrested by Villefort for carrying that letter. Now, years later, Noirtier is paralyzed, and when he discovers that his beloved granddaughter is about to be forced by her parents into a marriage with Franz d'Epinay, the old man is horrified because we discover later that Noirtier was the person who killed Franz' father years ago in a political duel. Noirtier is also aware, even though he is paralyzed, that Valentine is being used by Madame de Villefort because of Valentine's wealth, and therefore, Noirtier decides to cut her out of his will for her own protection. Shortly, his fears will be proven to be entirely correct as we see that Madame Villefort tries to poison Valentine so that Valentine's money will revert to her father, who will leave everything to his son.

Coincidences abound in Romantic novels, so the readers should not be surprised to discover that Caderousse, who now reappears in the plot, was an old cellmate of young Benedetto. Their relationship will lead directly to the death of Caderousse because of Caderousse's extreme greed.

The Count continues his plan of exacting slow and deliberate punishment for those guilty of causing him such extreme torment and suffering. Thus, he gives the party at his chateau in Auteuil, fully aware of the horrors perpetrated there by Villefort and the Baroness Danglars. As he shows them the rooms and projects stories about one of the rooms, he is actually describing the birth of the infant child that the Baroness had by Villefort, and when he mentions how the workmen discovered the bones of an infant child buried in the garden, he is of course referring to the child of the Baroness and Villefort. His

punishment is directed toward both the Baroness Danglars and Villefort, and the reader should repress all sympathy for these two people –
for they are *guilty* of bearing an illegitimate child and then of attempting to kill it by burying it alive.

The Count further involves Danglars in financial intrigues by
using his loyal friend Jacopo (the person who saved the Count from
drowning alongside the smuggling ship) to borrow large sums from
Danglars and thus having established excellent credit, to borrow a
million francs and then disappear. At the end of this section, the Count
causes further dissension by revealing to Danglars the means whereby
he can obtain damaging information about Morcerf's activities during
his Greek campaigns in Yanini, the campaigns which allowed him
to become so immensely wealthy and powerful. By the end of this
section, therefore, the Count has set into motion many different tech-
niques by which his enemies will all be entrapped.

Chapters 39–44

DEATH BY POISONING

Summary

When Danglars saw his wife leaving in her carriage – without
Debray – he never suspected that she was leaving to meet her old
lover, Villefort. Of course, however, *she* never suspected the extent
of the bad news which Villefort would have for *her*. Villefort tells her
very straightforwardly that they are both in extremely serious trouble.
He reminds her that Monte Cristo mentioned a baby's skeleton having
been unearthed. That would have been impossible, Villefort says,
because while he was burying the newborn baby, he was stabbed
by a Corsican and left for dead. Afterward, he was critically ill for
three months, but when he was able to travel, he returned to Auteuil
and dug up the entire garden area, searching for the makeshift casket.
There was no casket nor was there a baby's corpse. Someone dug it
up and is now waiting to make them both pay for their crime.

Madame Danglars screams: "You buried my child alive!" Villefort
loathes these accusations and tries to frighten her. Perhaps *she* talked
in her sleep . . . perhaps she is to blame. Whatever the reason for
their present predicament, someone *now* knows about them both. "We

are lost," he says. But he vows to discover who Monte Cristo is and why he lied about the baby's corpse being "accidentally" discovered — when indeed it was not.

Later, after Madame de Villefort and Valentine leave for a ball, Villefort shuts himself in his study. But before he has time to work at his papers, his former mother-in-law arrives. Her husband, Saint-Méran, has just died. The old lady is so distraught that Villefort has her put to bed, where she falls into a feverish sleep. When she rouses, she questions Villefort closely about Valentine's upcoming marriage. She is surprised that Franz, Valentine's fiancé, does not object to marrying the granddaughter of a fervent Bonapartist. After all, she says, Franz' father was assassinated only a few days before Napoleon returned from exile in Elba. Villefort tries to dismiss the old lady's worries; Franz, he says, was "only a child" when all that took place. Old Madame Saint-Méran, however, urges Villefort to marry his daughter to Franz as soon as possible. She says that she is certain that she is going to die. Last night, she saw a white "form" do something with her orangeade glass. And abruptly, she asks for the glass and empties it in a long, single swallow. An hour later, the old lady is dead.

Villefort is hysterical at the attending doctor's cross-examination. The old woman could not have died of poison, as the doctor states. Why would anyone want to poison her? Her sole heiress is Valentine — and Valentine is absolutely incapable of murder. But the doctor is *certain* not only that murder was committed, but that the poison used was brucine, a red liquid which he has been administering in very small doses to Villefort's father. One drop of that potion is a medicine; several drops are deadly poison.

Meanwhile, Valentine takes her beloved Maximilien to meet her grandfather, old Noirtier. He obviously approves of the young man as a husband for Valentine, but signals for them to wait, instead of eloping. He has plans for them.

Two days later, Monsieur and Madame de Saint-Méran are buried in a vault beside Renée, Valentine's mother. Then Villefort makes immediate plans for his daughter's marriage to Franz d'Epinay. The formal papers are ready to be signed when a message arrives from Villefort's father, old Noirtier. He wishes to see Franz immediately. So Franz, Valentine, and Villefort all hurry to the old man's room. There, by means of eye signals, a secret packet of old papers, tied in a black ribbon, is brought forth from Noirtier's desk. Franz is directed to read the papers.

He cries out when he sees that they are dated on the very day that his father was assassinated. There was, he reads, a secret club of Bonapartists during Louis XVIII's reign. Unfortunately, it was erroneously believed that Franz' father was a secret Bonapartist, and thus he was blindfolded one day and taken to one of the secret meetings of the Bonapartists. Among the matters discussed were the details of Bonaparte's return, including the mention of a certain letter carried on Morrel's ship, the *Pharaon* (the ship on which we first met Edmond Dantès. This "message" was also the message which Danglars used to indict Dantès and send him to prison for fourteen long, torturous years).

When Franz' father could no longer listen to plans for overthrowing the king's government, he spoke out loudly and said that his loyalty would *always* be to Louis — never to Bonaparte. Thus he was blindfolded again and was taken away and forced to fight a fair duel with old Noirtier, who killed him honorably. D'Epinay's death was no assassination.

Franz sinks lifelessly into a chair. The grandfather of his fiancée killed his own father! Villefort opens the door and flees in order not to choke the life out of his mute old father, who has just ruined Valentine's chance for marrying the wealthy Franz d'Epinay.

But Valentine, happy and frightened at the same time, kisses her grandfather and goes to the iron grill to speak of what has happened to her beloved Maximilien. "We're saved," she tells him, but she states that she will not reveal the full story until she is his wife.

Next day, Monsieur Noirtier has a new will made up, leaving Valentine his entire fortune. Valentine will soon be a very rich woman, with three hundred thousand francs a year.

Meanwhile, just as Valentine is planning for her marriage to Maximilien, another proposed marriage is being shattered. Morcerf (Fernand) comes to discuss his son's upcoming marriage to Eugénie Danglars with Danglars. Danglars tells Morcerf that "certain new circumstances have arisen"; Eugénie will *not* marry Albert. Morcerf proudly bites his lip at Danglars' arrogance. He asks for an explanation. "Be grateful that I don't give you one," snarls Danglars.

For a very short time, Maximilien is a very happy man. He is so very much in love with Valentine that he is scarcely able to believe in his happiness, expecially as he listens to Valentine tell him about the details of her future plans. Her grandfather has given her and Maximilien his blessing and, in eighteen months, Valentine will be of legal age and can marry Maximilien.

Just then, Valentine notices that Noirtier's old servant, Barrois, who has been standing in the background, is looking very tired. She offers him a glass of lemonade from her grandfather's tray. Gratefully, he empties the glass. In a few moments, he begins to stagger and his facial muscles begin to twitch violently. "Call the doctor," cries Valentine. D'Avrigny comes at once. Barrois rallies briefly, but then he is seized with an attack even more intense than the first one. The doctor discovers that Barrois has drunk some of the lemonade meant for Noirtier, and after Barrois falls dead with a loud cry, d'Avrigny reminds Villefort that the Saint-Mérans *also* died suddenly – and, moreover, that Madame Saint-Méran died of brucine poisoning, the same poison that has just now killed Barrois. Villefort cries out. But d'Avrigny says that he knows the symptoms of brucine poisoning very well. He performs a colored paper test and proves that brucine was indeed used.

"Death is in my house!" moans the public prosecutor. The doctor corrects him. "*Murder* is in your house," he says. Only the fact that Noirtier was taking graduated doses of brucine saved him, the doctor states. By accident, Noirtier was immune. But clearly, d'Avrigny believes that the poison was meant for Noirtier – and the evidence points to Valentine because *she* prepared the lemonade and would gain all of Noirtier's fortune if he were dead.

Villefort is furious with the doctor, but d'Avrigny is unmoved. He simply washes his hands of the Villeforts. If Villefort harbors criminals, or murderers, in his home, he wants nothing more to do with the family. He bids Villefort a final goodbye.

Commentary

This section continues the involvements which began earlier – that is, the complications before the plot begins to resolve itself. For example, the Count's plan to slowly become involved with his enemies in order to manipulate matters so that they, the enemies, begin to suffer has already been extremely effective. Madame Danglars meets with Villefort the next day in order to relive some of the horrors that they had originally perpetrated when Villefort tried to bury their son alive. But Villefort is even more concerned now because he knows that the Count did *not* discover the body of an infant; after Villefort recovered from the stab wounds, he returned to the garden and dug up the entire area, and he has lived all these years with the knowledge that his and Madame Danglars' son is alive somewhere in this world. Madame Danglars is horrified that Villefort would sink so low as to try to bury their child alive, and the grisly irony will soon be made clear when their son (once, supposedly dead) becomes unofficially engaged to Eugénie Danglars, his half-sister.

With the deaths of the Marquis de Saint-Méran and then of Barrois, evil in the Villefort household is beginning to assert itself. In both deaths, Doctor d'Avrigny suspects the use of poison—brucine—which the Count of Monte Cristo had talked about earlier to Madame Héloise de Villefort and had obliged her by sending her some. But in both deaths, it was Valentine who unknowingly administered the fatal potion, and finally, with the death of Barrois, it seems frighteningly clear to Doctor d'Avrigny that once again, Valentine is involved, because she brought the drink to her grandfather, old Noirtier, and Barrois accidentally drank it. All of the circumstantial evidence points to Valentine as the culprit in the deaths of these three old people. The doctor believes that the poison was intended for Villefort's father so that Valentine could inherit all of her maternal and paternal grandparents' monies. This causes Villefort to undergo deep and desperate grief—but not nearly so deep and desperate as Edmond Dantès underwent during his fourteen years of imprisonment.

Since Valentine is in love with Maximilien Morrel, but is honorably engaged to young Franz d'Epinay, there must be a way to honorably break the engagement. To do so, Noirtier reveals through some old documents that date back to 1815 that it was he who, for political reasons, killed Franz' father in an honorable duel over a difference in political philosophy. Thus, when Franz sends a letter breaking off the engagement, this is another blow, another bit of suffering for Villefort. The Count of Monte Cristo's desire for long and slow revenge is gradually being effected.

Chapters 45–46

THE DEATH OF CADEROUSSE

Summary

Andrea Cavalcanti returns to his hotel and discovers that Caderousse has been there looking for him. Moreover, Caderousse refused to take his "allowance." Reading the note that Caderousse left, Andrea fears that Caderousse plans to make trouble. He is right. Caderousse wants to see Andrea immediately. Therefore, Andrea dons a disguise and goes immediately to Caderousse's room.

Caderousse demands more money, and Andrea refuses him. Caderousse says that if Andrea really wanted more money, he could easily get it from Monte Cristo, his benefactor. Then, suddenly inspired by the thought of the wealthy Monte Cristo, Caderousse begins to question Andrea in detail about Monte Cristo's house on the Champs Elysées; Andrea answers in detail, and it is very clear that Caderousse means to rob Monte Cristo's house.

The two men part, and the next day, Monte Cristo receives a note informing him that his house will be robbed and, furthermore, that the thief will try and break into the desk in the Count's dressing room. The note ends with the information that this thief will be no ordinary thief; this thief will be an "enemy" of the Count. Monte Cristo's curiosity is sufficiently aroused so that he sets a trap.

He wants all of his staff moved to his house in Auteuil, and he wants the house on the Champs Elysées left exactly as it is – except that the shutters on the ground floor are to be closed. When that is finished, Monte Cristo and Ali slip into a side door and go up to Monte Cristo's bedroom to wait. It is half-past nine. At a quarter to twelve, Monte Cristo hears a faint noise, then another, and then a third; then he hears the sound of a diamond cutting the four sides of a pane of glass. (This is the diamond from a ring that Caderousse finagled from Andrea.)

Monte Cristo signals to Ali, and in the near-darkness, they see a man entering through an open window. He is alone. Ali touches the Count's shoulders, Outside, another man has climbed onto a hitching post to watch. Meanwhile, the thief methodically goes about his work, trying to unlock the desk with his collection of "nightingales" (assorted keys). Unable to find the correct key, Caderousse turns on a dim light. Monte Cristo can scarcely believe his eyes. He motions to Ali not to use any weapons. Quickly then, he dons his disguise as the Abbé Busoni, and taking a lighted candle, he steps into the room. "Good evening, Monsieur Caderousse," he says.

Caderousse is speechless. The Abbé wonders aloud why Caderousse is trying to rob the Count's house. Has prison taught him nothing? Clearly, he says, Caderousse is still very much himself— that is, he is Caderousse the murderer, referring to the jeweler who bought the diamond which Abbé Busoni gave to Caderousse and who was later killed because of the diamond. Caderousse, the Abbé infers, always wants *more*. Earlier, he wanted the enormous diamond *and* the money, so he killed the jeweler. Now, he is breaking into the home of a very wealthy gentleman.

"It was poverty," Caderousse gasps, "Poverty drove me to all this." No, Monte Cristo tells him. Poverty does *not* drive a man to use a *diamond* to cut through the pane of a window. Caderousse pleads for pity, and the Abbé offers him pity if he will but tell the truth. Caderousse agrees, and he begins to tell the Abbé about his years in prison, but when he begins to describe his relationship with Benedetto, he begins to lie, and so the Abbé *forces* him to confess what Andrea's role is in deceiving Parisian society. The Abbé states that he will reveal the truth about Andrea's fraudulence. Caderousse panics; if the Abbé does that, Caderousse will have no more money. Drawing a knife, he lunges at the Abbé, striking him in the middle of the chest, but the knife bounces back, its point blunted. Monte Cristo wore a metal vest, expecting this very thing. Monte Cristo then wrenches Caderousse's arm until he agrees to write a letter to Danglars exposing Andrea. Then he releases Caderousse, who climbs out of the window. During his escape, he is stabbed three times. He makes no sound; he simply slumps to the ground.

Slowly and painfully raising himself on one elbow, he calls out for the Abbé. Monte Cristo comes and forces Caderousse to write one more note, this time naming Benedetto as the man who stabbed him. Caderousse does so, then looks at the Abbé and accuses him of allowing Benedetto to stab him. Not I, says the Count, it was "the justice of God in Benedetto's hand." He tells Caderousse that God gave him health, good work, and good friends and that he squandered them all in laziness and drunkenness.

"I need a doctor," cries Caderousse, "not a priest!" Monte Cristo continues: "God sent an enormous diamond to you, and you became a murderer when you sought to double your good fortune. In prison, you were given a chance to escape and begin a new life when you were slipped a file by myself, but once free, you blackmailed Benedetto, then tried to rob Monte Cristo's house. Then you tried to kill *me!*"

He urges Caderousse to repent, but Caderousse refuses. So Monte Cristo takes off his disguise and orders Caderousse to look long and hard at him. "Oh, my God," Caderousse cries out, "Forgive me, Lord!"

Ten minutes later, the Abbé Busoni is found praying for the soul of the deceased.

Commentary

We saw earlier that Caderousse is a person of exceptional greed, and that the Count of Monte Cristo has given him ample opportunity to revise his values. But greed is too strong within Caderousse. Thus, he not only uses his knowledge of Benedetto's prison background, but he also uses his knowledge of Benedetto's fraudulent deception of the Count in order to gain access to the Count's house.

Benedetto, however, is as vicious a criminal as Caderousse is. While he is seemingly willing to betray his benefactor by giving Caderousse the floor plans of the count's house, he in turn informs the Count about Caderousse's intended break-in. And not content with these basic provisions, he later follows Caderousse to the Count's house, and when Caderousse does try and escape, he stabs his former fellow criminal.

When the Count recognizes Caderousse as the thief, he quickly changes to his disguise as the Abbé Busoni, taking the precaution to add heavy metal armor under his priestly frock. Thus, when Caderousse turns on the Abbé, his benefactor, and tries to kill him, the Count realizes that there is *no hope* for Caderousse. As the Count earlier maintained, he always wanted to play the role of Providence — meting out rewards and punishments. Now, the Count, in the disguise of the Abbé, allows Caderousse to leave, knowing full well that someone is lying in wait for Caderousse. Monte Cristo is, as it were, leaving everything to Providence. He tells Caderousse: "I want what God wants. . . . If you arrive home safely, leave Paris, leave France, and wherever you are, and as long as you behave honestly, I'll see that

you receive a small pension, because *if* you arrive home safely, then
. . . I'll believe that God has forgiven you, and I'll forgive you also."
The Count/Abbé cannot bring himself to actually kill Caderousse, but
he is willing to leave Caderousse's fate to the hands of Providence.

Before Monte Cristo allows Caderousse to leave, he forces him
to write a letter to Danglars, revealing that Andrea Cavalcanti is really
the criminal known as Benedetto; this will be a letter which will cause
intense pain for another of the Count's enemies. Once again, we will
see the Count effecting punishment by slow suffering, which he
believes his victims deserve. After the stabbing, the Count gets a
signed confession from Caderousse that Benedetto was the person who
stabbed him. Thus, the Count has now further entrapped yet another
of his enemies.

Before Caderousse dies, Monte Cristo tells him about his immoral-
ity, of the many opportunities he had to become a good and honest
man and about the many men whom he betrayed; then Monte Cristo
reveals that he is really Edmond Dantès, one of the oldest friends
whom Caderousse has betrayed. Caderousse is finally able to view
Monte Cristo as a savior, someone far superior to most earthly men.
He says, "You are the father of men in heaven and the judge of men
on earth. I refused to acknowledge you for so long, O my God! Forgive
me, Lord, forgive me." It is as though he is seeing in the Count the
aura of divine justice; then he dies, ending a chapter in the life of
one of Monte Cristo's oldest enemies.

Chapters 47–54

THE DEATH OF MORCERF

Summary

One morning, Albert and Beauchamp (the journalist) call on
Monte Cristo, and it is soon clear to the Count that Albert is out of
sorts, so he invites him to go away with him to his new estate in
Normandy, on the coast of France. Albert accepts the invitation, and
when he arrives there, he is once more in awe of the Count – and
of his new estate. From the terrace overlooking the sea, Albert sees
Monte Cristo's yacht, proudly at anchor in the bay. That night, Albert
falls asleep, lulled by the sound of waves breaking on the shore.

The following day, after shooting a dozen pheasants and catching a number of trout, Albert's idyllic interlude is cut short. Albert's valet arrives breathlessly from Paris, utterly exhausted from having traveled so far so quickly; he has a letter of urgent importance. Albert reads the first few lines and half-collapses. Monte Cristo murmurs omnisciently that "the sins of the father shall be visited upon the children." His insight is uncanny. The true identity of Albert's father has been revealed in the Paris press, as well as the fact that years ago when Fernand (de Morcerf) was supposedly defending Ali Pasha's fortress, he betrayed Ali Pasha to the Turks. (We learn later that not only did Fernand betray Ali Pasha, but that he assassinated him.) The implication is that "Count" de Morcerf (who bought his title), a member of the French Parliament, is both a *traitor* and a *fraud*. Albert leaves immediately for Paris. He is terribly confused. His father has such public stature that this scandal, he fears, will soon "echo all over Europe." He is correct.

Albert's father, meanwhile, reports to the Chamber totally unaware of the incriminating article that has just been published. Within minutes, one of his peers opens the floor for debate on the matter of Ali Pasha's assassination and what role Colonel Fernand Mondego (Morcerf's real name) played in it. Morcerf pales immediately, and then his entire body is rocked with a horrible shudder. There is a unanimous demand for an immediate investigation into the entire matter, and that evening, Morcerf presents himself before a twelve-member commission. His defense is that he was Ali Pasha's most trusted confidant; to be accused of betrayal is a grave error, for Morcerf *tried* to defend Ali Pasha, he says, but found him dead and his wife and daughter gone. Furthermore, he resents this *anonymous* attack on his honor.

The commission then produces a witness to substantiate the charges against Morcerf. Monte Cristo's slave-girl, Haydée, offers as evidence her birth certificate and her "bill of sale." She is Ali Pasha's daughter, she says, sold by Fernand (de Morcerf) to a slave merchant after her father was assassinated. At last, she says, she has the opportunity to avenge her father's murder. She identifies Morcerf by saying that her father's assassin has a wide scar on his right hand; immediately, Morcerf hides his hand and sinks into a chair, crushed by despair. Then, tearing open his coat, he flees from the room. Within moments, the commission finds him guilty of felony, treason, and dishonor.

When Albert hears of this decision, he vows to "find the de-nouncer" of his father. Beauchamp, the journalist, mentions that Danglars recently questioned his "correspondent" in the East about Ali Pasha's betrayal. Albert seizes on the news with vehemence and anger. He will fight Danglars, he says, and either he or Danglars "will be dead before the end of this day."

At first, Danglars shrinks with fear when he is confronted by Albert, but when he realizes that Albert's anger is totally irrational, he very cleverly suggests that it is Monte Cristo who is to blame for Albert's father's defamation. It was Monte Cristo, he says, who told him to investigate "the Ali Pasha affair" – which he did – and reported his findings to Monte Cristo immediately. Albert realizes that Danglars sounds like a man who has been used only as a "tool," and so he vows to go immediately to Monte Cristo and confront him with the charges.

The Count is unavailable when Albert calls, but Albert is told that Monte Cristo plans to go to the opera that evening, so Albert decides to attend the opera also and therefore sends word to Franz, Debray, and Maximilien to meet him there. He plans to use them as witnesses. Later, Albert questions his mother, Mercédès, about Monte Cristo. Mercédès cannot believe what her son tells her; she pleads with him to stay with her instead of going to the opera, but she is unsuccessful.

Monte Cristo arrives late, but Albert sees him enter, and during the intermission, he hurries to Monte Cristo's box. He shouts threats at the Count and makes an ugly scene, but Monte Cristo is undaunted; if Albert wants to duel, he will oblige him. He promises Maximilien that he will kill Albert tomorrow. Then he sits back and enjoys the rest of the opera.

Later, Mercédès visits Monte Cristo and agonizingly pleads for her son's life; then it is clear that she knows that Monte Cristo is Edmond Dantès. She begs him for pity – because of her. The Count refuses, revealing what a villain Fernand was – to help send Monte Cristo to prison for fourteen long, torturous years. Mercédès pleads with him, "the man [she] still loves," *not* to become the murderer of her son. Finally, Monte Cristo agrees not to kill Albert. Instead, he tells Mercédès, he will allow Albert to kill *him*. Gratefully, Mercédès leaves Monte Cristo. The Count is puzzled by Mercédès' seeming in-difference to his own, certain death. He curses the day that he vowed to revenge himself on his enemies.

Next morning, Maximilien (Monte Cristo's "second") and Emmanuel

(Julie Morrel's husband) arrive for Monte Cristo. They tell the Count that he will fire first, since he is "the offended party." Maximilien fears that Monte Cristo is not a good shot, and so the Count attaches an ace of diamonds to a plank and instantly shoots *each* of the four corners of the diamond in the center of the card. Maximilien cries out to the Count for mercy for Albert, but seemingly, the Count's decision will not be swayed. Yet, he says, despite the marksmanship that Maximilien has just seen, it will be Monte Cristo, and *not Albert,* who will be carried back.

The three men arrive at the appointed hour, and when Albert arrives — at a full gallop — he leaps off his horse and, before his own witnesses, he apologizes for his conduct. He knows now that his father, Fernand Mondego, *did* betray Ali Pasha. But, far worse than that was his father's betrayal of Edmond Dantès. Because of the enormity of Fernand's crime, Albert can only thank Monte Cristo for not deciding on more painful vengeance than he did.

Monte Cristo realizes that Mercédès has told her son everything; obviously she planned to do so all along, after Monte Cristo promised *not* to kill Albert. The two men shake hands on Albert's apology, and Albert returns home and begins to pack his belongings, including the portrait of Mercédès as a Catalan fisherwoman. But he discovers, to his surprise, that his mother is *also* packing. The two vow to make a complete break with their pasts, and Mercédès advises Albert to use the name of "Herrera," her father's name, instead of Morcerf.

Albert replies that if Monte Cristo was able to endure his own misery, unhappiness, and injustice, then he, Albert, can do the same. So he and his mother make ready to leave. Just then, Bertuccio, Monte Cristo's steward, delivers a letter to Albert from the Count. Albert is told to claim three thousand francs (money which Edmond Dantès buried twenty-two years ago, when he believed that he would marry Mercédès); the money lies buried in the garden of Dantès' father's house in Marseilles. Mercédès reads the letter and accepts the Count's offer. She'll take the money to a convent with her.

At home, Monte Cristo learns that Maximilien is deeply in love with someone, and so he tells him goodbye and asks him not to forget to call on the Count if ever the need arises. Maximilien agrees to do so. Shortly thereafter, Morcerf (Fernand) arrives to speak with Monte Cristo. He wants verification that his son actually *apologized* to Monte Cristo — instead of dueling with him. He cannot understand why.

Because, Monte Cristo says, "there was another man guiltier than I." Monte Cristo then names Fernand, labeling him an "enemy." Fernand challenges Monte Cristo to a duel, this time with swords. But Monte Cristo first identifies Fernand for *what* he is: Fernand, he says, deserted the French army on the eve of Waterloo; he served as a spy in Spain; he assassinated Ali Pasha, and he unscrupulously managed to become Count Morcerf. Fernand is livid. He demands to know who Monte Cristo is so that he can pronounce his name aloud as he plunges his sword into the Count's heart. Monte Cristo leaves the room and returns dressed as a young sailor. Morcerf's teeth begin to chatter; he leans against the wall, and then he slides out of the room, crying out in terror, *"Edmond Dantès!"*

Fernand returns home just in time to see his wife and son leaving together. Their carriage door closes, and Fernand is alone. Moments later, a shot rings out so violently that one of the frames in the bedroom window is shattered.

Commentary

These chapters show how the Count effects his plan for revenge against his old enemy, Fernand, the man responsible for mailing the letter which imprisoned Dantès for fourteen years. His first act is to remove Fernand's son, Albert, from the environs so that Fernand will not be able to turn to his "beloved son" for solace. We see again the Count's very strong religious belief that the "sins of the father shall be visited upon the children to the third or fourth generation." Consequently, all the time that Monte Cristo has been seeing Albert, he has remained aloof, knowing that this young man, however charming, is nevertheless the son of one of his most detested enemies.

The damaging information about Morcerf's treacherous behavior at the battle of Yanina and his betrayal of his benefactor (Ali Pasha) is information that was given to the press by Danglars, partly because Danglars has never liked Count de Morcerf – even when they were young together and especially since the Count was able to buy a higher title than the one that Baron Danglars has. But more important, Danglars wants some reason to break off the marriage between Albert and Eugénie Danglars because he wants to align himself with a much larger fortune through young Andrea Cavalcanti, but who (unbeknownst to Danglars) is an imposter as well as the illegitimate son of Danglars' wife.

These chapters show that the Count's carefully laid plans are now beginning to pay off. We must, therefore, review the Count's philosophy: if a man has made you suffer for an untold number of years, then you are not right in revenging yourself instantaneously; you are obligated, as it were, to make your enemy endure prolonged suffering. Thus, Count de Morcerf must first face the humiliations of being called a traitor in the newspaper, of being charged to defend himself before the Chamber of Deputies (of which he is a very proud and feared member), and then he must face the direct accusations of Haydée, whom Morcerf obtained by treachery when he betrayed Haydée's father, then sold her as a slave girl, along with her mother, who soon died. Moreover, he must hear the Chamber of Deputies vote him guilty by a unanimous voice vote. He is now a man in *complete* public disgrace.

If the reader will remember that this is a Romantic novel, written for an audience believing in personal honor and integrity, then Albert de Morcerf's actions against the Count of Monte Cristo won't seem so strange. It is not that Albert ever questions his father's dishonorable actions – all noble families have things to hide – but it is dishonorable for any man to make public these dishonorable actions. Thus, Albert feels that Monte Cristo is totally accountable: Albert remembers that Monte Cristo knew everything, for he bought Ali Pasha's daughter, and then knowing everything about the "Ali Pasha" affair, he urged Danglars to write to Yanina. Finally, he took Albert to Normandy with him just at the moment when he knew the disaster was to occur. Thus, it now seems to Albert that Monte Cristo planned everything and that he was in league "with his father's enemies."

When Albert questions his mother about his father's enemies, he wonders about Monte Cristo because the Count has "always refused to eat or drink anything in our house . . . and as you know, Mother, the Count is almost an Oriental and, in order to maintain full freedom to avenge themselves, Orientals never eat or drink anything in the house of an enemy." Now, earlier scenes in the novel (often omitted in abridged versions), in which the Countess de Morcerf (Mercédès) would pick grapes and offer them to the Count who refused, or when Mercédès would bring the Count tempting morsels which he would always refuse, become clear when we realize why Monte Cristo always refused to eat what was offered to him. Note too, that in this present scene, when Mercédès comes to plead with the Count for the life of her son, this is not by any means the first time that they have acknowledged by indirect signs that they are indeed the old lovers of years ago, but this is the first time that they call each other by their real names. When Mercédès tells Monte Cristo that Albert attributes Fernand's misfortunes to him, the Count reiterates his basic belief: "What has happened to his father is *not* a misfortune: It's a *punishment*. I haven't struck him down: Providence has punished him." Thus, as with the death of Caderousse, the Count believes strongly in the efficacy of Providence. When Mercédès pleads for the life of her son, the Count tells her of Fernand's betrayal and says that he, Monte Cristo, is only acting in the name of God – "You're asking me to disobey God, who brought me back from a living death in order to punish them. Impossible . . . I suffered for fourteen years, I wept and cursed for fourteen years, and now I tell you, Mercédès, I must have vengeance!"

Finally, the remembrance of Monte Cristo's past love for Mercédès conquers his desire for vengeance; Monte Cristo agrees not to kill Albert, but he lets it be known to Mercédès, and later to Maximilien, that he *will* allow Albert to kill him. This is the only *honorable* course that he can take, for no longer can he adhere to his credo that the "sins of the father must be visited upon the son."

Fernand's death comes after he has confronted the Count with a demand for a duel; when the Count reveals that he is Edmond Dantès, Fernand can barely stagger home, and when he arrives there, he discovers that his wife and son – the only people whom he has ever loved – have totally rejected him and are leaving his house, carrying absolutely nothing that belongs to him. With this knowledge, Fernand shoots himself, thus ridding the Count of Monte Cristo of the second of his four enemies.

Chapters 55 – 67

THE MADNESS OF VILLEFORT

Summary

Leaving Monte Cristo, Maximilien walks to the Villefort residence. He meets Valentine and is immediately concerned about her health. She seems disoriented. Valentine tells him that she is "slightly indisposed," but that she is gaining strength; she has been taking slow, but increasing doses of her grandfather's medicine (brucine). She says that she'll be fine; only minutes ago, she drank a glass of sugared water.

Madame Danglars and Eugénie arrive to announce Eugénie's engagement to "Prince" Cavalcanti, a title that somehow "sounds better" to Madame Danglars than does "Count." Eugénie protests her engagement; she does *not* look forward to marriage and becoming "a wife or a slave of a man." She wants to be free, and she *needs* to be free, she says. Valentine leaves the room and collapses on the landing, where Maximilien finds her and carries her to old Noirtier's room. There, Valentine suffers another attack, and this time she becomes so cold and so lifeless that Doctor d'Avrigny is called.

Maximilien goes immediately to Monte Cristo. He says that he fears that Valentine has been murdered. Monte Cristo instructs Maximilien to "be strong" and not to "lose hope."

Back at the Villefort residence, Doctor d'Avrigny announces guardedly that Valentine is still alive, and Villefort suggests that Valentine be put in her own bed. Then he exits. Doctor d'Avrigny stays behind with Noirtier and questions the old gentleman about Barrois' (Noirtier's servant's) death. Noirtier tells the doctor, with signs, that Valentine was poisoned by the same person who killed Barrois, and moreover, that Barrois was poisoned *by accident;* he drank a glass of liquid that was meant for Noirtier. The doctor then asks Noirtier if it was he who began giving Valentine increasingly potent doses of brucine – to make her immune if someone tried to poison her. Noirtier signals *Yes,* it was indeed he. The doctor leaves then and goes to Valentine's room, where he discovers an Italian priest – Abbé Busoni (Monte Cristo, in disguise).

Three days later, the Danglars' mansion is all aglitter with guests adorned with diamonds, rubies, and other precious stones. Eugénie Danglars is announcing her engagement to young Cavalcanti to an enormous crowd of her father's friends. At exactly nine o'clock, Monte Cristo arrives and soon after, a notary calls for the signing of the wedding contract.

Baron Danglars signs, then hands the pen to the representative of Major Cavalcanti (the Major himself has disappeared). Madame Danglars sighs; she wishes that Monsieur Villefort were here, whereupon Monte Cristo steps up and says that, unfortunately, he is the cause of Villefort's absence. Andrea Cavalcanti (Benedetto) immediately pricks up his ears. Monte Cristo continues, and he says that the vest on the murdered Caderousse has been examined and that a piece of paper was found in one of the pockets. It was a letter addressed to Baron Danglars. Monte Cristo speculates that the letter might have concerned a plot against Danglars, so he sent the vest and the letter to the public prosecutor, Villefort.

The notary then announces that the signing of the contract will once again resume; just then, an officer and two gendarmes enter the salon and ask for Andrea Cavalcanti, "an escaped convict accused of murdering another escaped convict by the name of Caderousse." A search begins for young Cavalcanti, but he seems to have disappeared.

Upstairs, Eugénie makes plans to flee with her friend Louise d'Armilly. She says that she *loathes* men and intends to leave Paris immediately! Then she cuts off her long black hair and dons a man's suit of clothes. Louise is speechless at Eugénie's daring; they quickly hire a cab and escape into the night. Monsieur Danglars has lost his daughter.

"Andrea Cavalcanti" is a clever young man. Before escaping, he detours through the room where the "wedding jewels" are on display. He seizes the most valuable ones, then he cajoles a cab driver to whisk him as fast as possible out of the city (ostensibly to try and catch a friend in another carriage); then, after he alights, he smudges dust on one side of his overcoat and asks to rent a horse (his own horse threw him in the darkness, he says). All of his plans work, and by 4 a.m., he has settled himself in a rented room and is ready for a good sleep, after having consumed a cold chicken and some excellent wine. He is absolutely certain that no one will capture him, for he plans to depart early, travel through a forest, and then cross the French border.

Unfortunately, Andrea sleeps later than he expected to — and when he peers out the window, he sees three gendarmes arriving at the inn. Hastily, he writes a note to the innkeeper, making it sound as though he had to leave in shame because he had no money. He leaves a handsome tie pin behind as payment for board and room, then he climbs up the chimney and onto the roof. He is afraid, however, that while the gendarmes are searching the rooms in the inn, they might look out of an upper window and spy him on the roof. Thus, he slips down a chimney where there is no smoke. Imagine his surprise, when he drops down the chimney and onto the hearth of a bedroom — and two young ladies rise up out of their bed and scream for help. One of them is Eugénie Danglars – the woman he was supposed to marry – and the other is her friend Louise! Eugénie tells Andrea to climb back up the fireplace, but one of the gendarmes has already seen Andrea through the keyhole and breaks open the door and arrests him. Andrea is taken back to Paris and imprisoned.

Back at the Villefort residence, Valentine has still not recovered. She seems to see phantoms in her fevered, delirious state. One night in particular, she seems to see a human figure approaching her bed; the figure takes her drinking glass, samples the contents, then speaks: "Now you may drink." It is the Count of Monte Cristo. He explains to her that he has been keeping guard over her, ascertaining *who* has come into her room, *what food* has been prepared for her, and *what liquids* Valentine has been given to drink. He says that, just now, he emptied the glass by her bed – which was filled with poison – and refilled it with a therapeutic potion. Valentine is confused and distraught: Monte Cristo obviously knows *who* her poisoner is.

He does indeed, and he tells Valentine to pretend that she is asleep and she will see for herself who is trying to murder her. Then Monte Cristo hides.

Madame de Villefort, Valentine's twenty-five-year-old stepmother enters; she empties a flask into Valentine's glass, then silently withdraws. Valentine is dazed with horror and disbelief, as Monte Cristo explains Madame de Villefort's motives: when Valentine is dead, he says, the huge fortune that was to be Valentine's inheritance will revert to her father (Villefort), who will leave it all to Edouard – the one true love in Madame de Villefort's life. Valentine can scarcely believe that her stepmother is so diabolical, so she asks the Count what she must do. He tells her that "no matter what happens . . . if you awaken in a tomb or a coffin, keep your head and say, 'Maximilien is watching over me.' " Then he gives her a pill the size of a pea, bids her goodbye, and tells her that she is saved. Valentine gradually falls asleep, looking like "an angel lying at the foot of the lord."

In the morning, a nurse enters and shrieks. Seemingly, Valentine is dead. Villefort enters and sinks to the floor, his head on Valentine's bed. Madame de Villefort arrives and is speechless. She is *sure* that the glass by Valentine's bed was empty, but now it is one-third *full!* And Doctor d'Avrigny is studying it, she thinks, in order to punish her. D'Avrigny then makes a little experiment with a drop of nitric acid, and immediately, the potion changes color. "Aha!" he exclaims. Madame de Villefort crumples to the floor unconscious.

Maximilien appears and is transfixed; then he lifts up old Noirtier *and* his wheelchair and brings them both into Valentine's room. Noirtier looks as though he is on the verge of an epileptic seizure, and Maximilien vows that he will be Valentine's avenger. Villefort, in secret to Maximilien, confesses that he knows who the murderer is, and he asks for three days before Maximilien begins his vengeance. On his way out, the doctor sees Abbé Busoni, who agrees to attend to all last rites. (Busoni, remember, is Monte Cristo in disguise.)

Next day, Monte Cristo visits Danglars and asks for five million francs. Danglars, who has been boasting about the immense fortune of his firm, is panic-stricken, but finally he pays the Count, who leaves. Within moments, Monsieur de Boville is announced, and *he also* asks for five million francs from Danglars; tomorrow, his books are being examined. Danglars promises to have the money ready by noon the next day. Of course, however, he won't. He writes a letter to his wife, then takes about fifty thousand francs, his passport, and closes the door behind him.

Valentine's funeral procession is especially painful for Maximilien, and afterward, he retires to his room, lays out his pistols, and begins to write a suicide note. He is interrupted by Monte Cristo, who successfully begs him not to commit suicide. The Count tells him to *live* — with hope. Then, as proof of his compassion for Maximilien's future, he reveals who he actually is — Edmond Dantès, the "savior" of the Morrel shipping firm. Dantès says that within a week, all matters which now seem hopeless will be resolved. Then, in exactly one month, they will meet and be happier than Maximilien can even imagine. Maximilien agrees to Monte Cristo's proposition and also to his invitation to move into the Count's house with him.

Coincidentally, Albert and Mercédès have chosen to live in a rooming house that contains an apartment that is being used by Debray and Madame Danglars for their affair. Madame Danglars assures Debray that her husband's farewell note is final. He will *never* return to Paris nor to her. She has been abandoned. Debray becomes very nervous. He reminds her that she is rich, rich beyond measure, and then, business-like, he announces that it is time for them to reconcile their individual financial balances. At this point, Madame Danglars carefully conceals the pain which Debray's words give her and hurries away, scorning him for allowing her to leave "like a servant with a paycheck."

Upstairs, Albert tells his mother that he has enlisted in France's military forces. She sobs out of fear for him, but Albert manages to get her to promise that she will "live to hope." He will henceforth use her maiden name in his new life, and he tells her further to make plans to go to Marseilles and claim the money which Edmond Dantès saved long ago and buried to be used after he was married to Mercédès.

From a secret vantage point, Monte Cristo wonders if he can ever bestow happiness on these innocent creatures who have, by association with him, become victims of his vengeance.

In the maximum security unit in the prison of La Force, Benedetto lives in great optimism. He is certain that Fortune will soon be kind to him.

Villefort continues to work feverishly on the legal case involving the murderer of Caderousse, and before he leaves for court, he asks his wife straightforwardly *where she keeps her poison*. She is thrown off-guard and tries to evade the question. Villefort then accuses her of murdering three people and of watching them die. But he tells her that "as public prosecutor" and because of the possibility that her execution would "taint the Villefort name," he will be merciful to her. He swears that he will administer only "justice." (We feel that he wants the poison in order to force her to drink it and thereby save him, Villefort, from a court scandal.) Madame Villefort falls at her husband's feet, and Villefort tells her that he must go; he is due in court to demand the death penalty for a murderer. If she is still alive when he returns home, he vows that she will be in prison by nightfall.

The "Benedetto Case" produces a great sensation all over Paris. Everyone, it seems, knows about "Cavalcanti"; his splendid adventures are recounted in copious detail in the newspapers, alongside stories about his life in prison. Because Benedetto is handsome and suave, most people believe that he is the living reincarnation of a Byronic hero and is the tragic victim of Injustice and Misunderstanding.

Benedetto's actual day in court, however, is far different from the Romantic gossip that surrounds him. He begins the session by confessing that he murdered Caderousse. He is asked his name, but he says that he cannot say what his name *really* is; he does not know. He only knows what his father's name is: that name is Villefort.

A thunderous explosion of surprise rocks the courtroom. Villefort slumps half-unconscious in his chair, and a woman in one corner of the courtroom faints (this is Madame Danglars, hidden behind a veil). Andrea still doesn't fully understand what is taking place. All he knows is that he was born in Auteuil, he says, on September 27, 1817, and that his father immediately picked him up, told his mother that her new baby was dead, and then buried the baby alive in the garden. Benedetto has learned these facts from a Corsican who stabbed Villefort, then opened the grave that Villefort had just deposited the baby into, and took the boy to his sister-in-law to raise. This baby was born with such a "perverse nature" that he grew up evil and turned to crime — loathing and cursing his father for condemning him to hell — "if he had not lived . . . and to poverty if — by a miracle — he lived." He still doesn't know who his mother is and he doesn't want to know.

A shrill cry arises from the courtroom, and the woman who fainted earlier succumbs to a violent fit of hysteria. As she is being carried from the courtroom, her veil falls aside: it is Madame Danglars.

"Look at Villefort! There is the proof!" Benedetto cries, pointing to the staggering, disheveled public prosecutor who has torn his cheeks with his fingernails. In a choked voice, his teeth chattering, Villefort confesses that everything that Benedetto has said is true. He, Villefort, is guilty. Then he lunges mindlessly out of the courtroom.

Villefort realizes that his life is now ruined. He writhes inside his carriage. He acted like a god of Justice to his wife; he sentenced her, as it were, to death. Now, trembling with terror and remorse, he realizes that Madame de Villefort became a criminal *only* because "she touched me" — in other words, his own criminal nature "infected her." And he dared to accuse and condemn *her!* He prays that she is still alive. They must flee from France immediately. The scaffold is waiting for them both.

Sighing with hope, he sees nothing amiss at home. He calls again and again to his wife, and finally he finds her, pale and staring at him from her boudoir. "It's done," she moans and falls to the floor. Desperately, Villefort calls out for Edouard. Icy sweat breaks out on his forehead, and his legs begin to tremble. He sees his son lying on a sofa in the boudoir. Villefort leaps over the corpse of his wife and fervently kisses Edouard's cold cheeks. The boy is dead.

At that moment, Abbé Busoni enters; he has come to pray for

Valentine's soul, he says. Villefort steps back in terror. The voice coming from the Abbé is *not* Busoni's. Monte Cristo tears off his disguise and stands before Villefort, daring him to recognize him. With an anguished shriek, Villefort acknowledges that the man before him is Edmond Dantès. "Is your vengeance complete?" he cries, grabbing Dantès' wrist and leading him to where Madame de Villefort and Edouard lie. Then he utters a loud shriek, followed by a burst of laughter, and runs down the stairs. Later, Monte Cristo sees him digging in the ground with a spade. "I must find my son," Villefort gasps. He is mad.

At home, Monte Cristo calls to Maximilien and tells him that they are leaving Paris tomorrow. He hopes that he hasn't caused any more suffering in his unrelenting quest for vengeance.

Commentary

This section, while focusing on the downfall of Villefort, also continues with Monte Cristo's slow and deliberate entrapment of Baron Danglars. Dumas leaves the scene of the Villefort family so that we can witness Danglars' slow and painful downfall. After everyone except Andrea Cavalcanti has signed the marriage contract before the huge gathering, Baron Danglars is told that the murdered man, an escaped convict, was carrying a letter addressed to the Baron, and that the murdered man's name is Caderousse. Upon hearing the name of his old fellow conspirator, Danglars is visibly upset, and then he is horrified when the police raid his house in search of young Cavalcanti — "an escaped convict from the prison at Toulon, and he's also accused of murdering another escaped convict by the name of Caderousse." The Baron is left in a state of consternation and shock. In addition to his crumbling financial structure, his entire social life has been slowly and painfully deteriorating. Now, it has collapsed before his eyes. His daughter, Eugénie, was forced into two unwanted engagements (first, to Albert de Morcerf, whose father is now dishonored; then, to Andrea Cavalcanti, who turned out to be a criminal), and she has taken advantage of the confusion to run away (by a circuitous route) to Rome so she can live the life of a free and unhampered artist. Thus, in addition to everything else, Baron Danglars has lost his only daughter.

Later in this section, Danglars will become desperately confused by his failing financial affairs, especially when Monte Cristo suddenly withdraws five million francs and, at the same time, Monsieur de Boville arrives to collect another five million francs owed to charity hospitals. In desperation, Baron Danglars embezzles all the money he can put his hands on and, totally disgraced, he leaves France – but with a considerable amount of money, money which he clearly worships more than he does his family.

This section focuses primarily on the destruction of Villefort, as we watch Monte Cristo's slow punishment erode Villefort's arrogance – first, he must endure the illness of his beloved daughter Valentine, and then, he must accept her "death," after Monte Cristo gives her a mysterious pill which puts her into a state resembling death. Villefort is deeply grieved and almost inconsolable upon hearing that his daughter is dead, and he must further face Maximilien's and Dr. d'Avrigny's charges that Valentine was murdered, in addition to enduring the disgrace of having "a crime committed in my own house." Villefort is also horrified to discover through his father, Monsieur Noirtier, that the murderess is *his own wife!* Then he must face the horror of confronting his wife and demanding her suicide – or else he will have her sentenced to public execution. He tells her, "I am going to the Palace of Justice now to demand the death penalty for a murderer. If I find you alive when I return, you will be in prison by nightfall."

In addition to Danglars' shock at the humiliating revelation that Andrea Cavalcanti (alias Benedetto) is a criminal, this news will bring about Villefort's total destruction, and it will further emphasize Monte Cristo's belief that "the sins of the father are visited upon the son" since the evil and corrupt Andrea is actually the son of Villefort; in addition, poetic justice can be seen in the fact that the son will accuse the father of attempting to bury him alive when he was an infant. This reveals to us that Villefort is capable of the most horrible sin and atrocity known to civilized man – that is, of coldly and deliberately burying one's own child alive. Poetic justice occurs when the son whom the father tried to kill returns to publicly destroy his own father. Ultimately, however, we must remember that the Count of Monte Cristo has arranged *all* of this for the sake of punishment and justice.

But Villefort's slow punishment is not yet complete. When he arrives home, repentant of his demand that his wife kill herself, he discovers that she has already taken the poison and is now dying.

The ultimate horror is revealed when Villefort discovers that his wife has also poisoned their son, who is already dead. Then Abbé Busoni, who is visiting Monsieur Noirtier, reveals that he is, first, the Count of Monte Cristo, and then he forces Villefort to recognize him as Edmond Dantès, whom Villefort "condemned to a slow and hideous death," thereby depriving Dantès "of love, freedom and fortune." Villefort is barely able to withstand the horror of it all. He leads Dantès to the dead young Edouard, asking him, "Is your vengeance now complete?" Villefort then loses his mind and wanders through the garden in complete madness, searching for his dead son. The Count has once again gained his revenge against yet another of his enemies.

This section shows the first basic and fundamental change in Monte Cristo; until now, he has functioned under the theory that "the sins of the father are visited upon" subsequent generations. For this reason, he would have dueled with and killed Albert de Morcerf because Albert is the son of a hated enemy, but Monte Cristo *did* see a certain nobility in Albert, in spite of his treacherous father. Likewise, when Maximilien asks Monte Cristo to help Valentine, the daughter of his dreaded enemy Villefort, Monte Cristo is horrified to discover that so noble a young man as Maximilien could love such a descendant: "You love Valentine? You love that daughter of a cursed breed?" And yet he, out of his devotion to the young Maximilien, is persuaded ultimately to devote himself to saving and preserving Valentine for Maximilien. Finally, when Monte Cristo is confronted with the death of the young nine-year-old Edouard de Villefort, he doubts "for the first time" that he has a right to do what he has done. He hopes that "God grant that I haven't done too much already." Monte Cristo now seems to be satiated with his desire for revenge, even though he has arranged for the final destruction of Danglars in the next section.

Chapters 68–72

THE COLLAPSE OF DANGLARS

Summary

As Monte Cristo and Maximilien leave Paris, the Count asks young Morrel if he regrets coming with him. Maximilien, of course, confesses his terrible and agonizing grief for Valentine, but Monte Cristo urges him to remember that, above all, the friends whom one loses to death are in our hearts forever – *not* in the earth. He asks Maximilien to give up his gloomy mood. The two men then make a sea journey that is characterized by one of the Count's passions – that is, speed. And even Maximilien allows himself to feel the intoxication of the wind in his hair.

After they have docked at Marseilles, Maximilien goes to the cemetery where his father is buried, and Monte Cristo goes to call on Mercédès, who is living in the house that Dantès' father once lived in. (Mercédès, we are told, found the money that Dantès buried twenty-four years before.) She is sitting in an arbor, weeping when the Count finds her. He tells her that Albert did the right thing when he joined the military service, that he will now become strong through adversity. Staying in Marseilles would only have made Albert bitter. Mercédès is profuse in her gratitude for all that Dantès has done, but he demurs; he was only an agent of God, he says, bringing disaster and suffering on the villains who were responsible for his captivity, his long years of imprisoned solitude, and his measureless sorrow. He is only a single part of a great design. He tells Mercédès that perhaps some day she will let him share his wealth with her, and she agrees to accept his generosity – but only with Albert's permission. Then she touches the Count's trembling hand and tells him *au revoir* (until we meet again) instead of goodbye. As she looks away toward the harbor, her eyes are not on the Count's slowly diminishing figure; instead, they are on a single, tiny ship far in the distance that carries her son away from her. Yet in her heart, a small voice murmurs, "Edmond! Edmond!"

Monte Cristo can think of only one thing; he may never see Mercédès again. Once, he was so cocksure and confident. Now he has doubts. Introspectively, he wonders if he was right to follow the trail of vengeance for ten years. But only briefly does he question his actions. He instantly delights in the beauty of the day, the sky, the boats, and the harbor. But again, the dark mood of memory envelops him as he recalls a certain ship in this very harbor, the ship that carried him away to the horrible prison of Chateau d'If.

The Count hires a nearby pleasure boat and has it take him to the old prison, which, since the July Revolution, has been used only as a curiosity of terror and punishment. It is empty now. A cold pallor sweeps through the Count as he steps ashore. He secures a guide and asks to be taken to his old cell. He is curious if there are any stories connected with this particular cell, and he is stunned to discover that he is filled with fear when he hears a complete stranger recount all of the details of the imprisonment of Edmond Dantès, "that dangerous man," and the details about the imprisonment of "a poor priest who went mad" (Faria). He listens in a cold sweat as his guide tells him about the secret passageway which the two men made, of Faria's illness and his death, and about Dantès' daring and ingenious escape from the supposedly inescapable Chateau d'If.

Monte Cristo asks to see the cell of this "poor, mad priest," and afterward, overcome with emotion, he tips the guide twenty-four gold francs (symbolically, one franc for every year since he was imprisoned). The guide is confused at such generosity, so he decides impulsively to show Monte Cristo "a sort of book written on scraps of cloth." This is the book that Faria painstakingly wrote, into which he poured all the treasures of his knowledge and wisdom. In it, Monte Cristo sees the phrase " 'Thou shalt tear out the teeth of the dragon and trample the lions underfoot,' sayeth the Lord." This, then, is holy proof! This is a sign that stills Monte Cristo's questioning heart. Here, God justifies and *demands* vengeance! He impulsively buys the book made from scraps and strips of cloth, puts ten thousand francs in a wallet, and makes the guide promise not to open the wallet until after he has departed. Then he calls to a boatman and orders him to sail for Marseilles immediately. His victory is complete! He has no more doubts.

Monte Cristo meets Maximilien, still in the cemetery, and tells him to meet him on the Isle of Monte Cristo on *the fifth of October*. A yacht will be waiting to take him there. Then, if Maximilien is still convinced that he must commit suicide because of his unrelieved suffering for Valentine, the Count will give him permission to die. He will even help him. But for now, he must *hope* and *live*. Monte Cristo bids him farewell.

Meanwhile, Monsieur Danglars is joyously making his escape from Paris. He secures five million francs from the firm of Thomson and French (Monte Cristo's firm), and note in this chapter who the employee is in the back room of the firm: it is Peppino, the handsome and tanned bandit whom Dantès secured a pardon for long ago. In addition, there is mention of Luigi Vampa, the bandit king who kidnapped Albert de Morcerf. Clearly, they are both a part of Monte Cristo's scheme to make Danglars (the former purser on the *Pharaon*) suffer for his part in unjustly imprisoning Edmond Dantès.

When Danglars finishes his banking transactions, a carriage is waiting for him, and he is whisked away from Rome just before nightfall; then the carriage halts and sets off again. Suddenly, Danglars realizes that he is being taken *back* to Rome. The carriage stops, and Danglars is ordered out. He is taken along a twisting route and into a cavern, half-open like an eyelid, and to a cell made from a hollowed-out rock. Obviously, his abductors do not mean to kill him, despite the fact that he recognizes the villainous Luigi Vampa among the bandits. He falls asleep that night confident that *if* he is ransomed, the sum will be paid.

In the morning, Danglars calls out for food, but, to his surprise, he learns that he must pay for it: 100,000 francs *per meal*. He tries to protest, and he tries to fast, but two weeks later, his cash flow is exhausted, and he is almost mad with hunger and frustration. What *do* they want from him? He thinks of death sometimes with longing; he is that miserable. Finally, when all of his money is gone, he begs Vampa for *only* the opportunity to live—here in these caves, if necessary. He wants only the opportunity to have enough to eat. He groans in pain, and then he hears a deep and solemn voice asking, "Do you repent?" The voice comes from a figure hidden in the shadows who is wearing a cloak. Danglars cries out that he *does repent!* Then Monte Cristo steps forth and forgives Danglars, but tells him that he, Monte Cristo, is *not* a Count. Instead, he is the man whom Danglars betrayed and dishonored years ago: he is Edmond Dantès.

Danglars gasps, cries out, and falls to the floor. When he recovers, he is free; he has been abandoned along the roadside. He bends down to drink from a brook and is stunned: his hair has turned white.

Commentary

In these chapters, Monte Cristo begins to put his life into its proper perspective. He bids farewell to Paris, believing that "the spirit of God led me there, and He has led me out triumphant. He alone knows that I now leave without hatred or pride, but not without regret; he alone knows that I have not used the power which He entrusted to me either for myself or for vain causes. Now my work is completed, my mission accomplished. Farewell, Paris, Farewell!" Then he visits Mercédès and leaves her with peace and understanding between them and with the implication that he will constantly watch over the future fortune of her son, Albert de Morcerf. He then visits the infamous Chateau d'If and after generously tipping the guide, he is given the book that Abbé Faria wrote on strips of cloth. His delight at finally possessing the Abbé's manuscript is immeasurable.

Then Dumas returns our attention to Monte Cristo's revenge against Danglars. If we remember that Fernand (Count de Morcerf) loved his wife and son more than anything else, and that his ultimate punishment occurred when they denied him and left his house empty-handed, and if we remember that Villefort cherished his public image and ambition more than anything else, and that ultimately he was publicly ruined, then we must also remember that Danglars loves nothing so much as he loves money. Consequently, Monte Cristo arranges matters so that Danglars is constantly losing money, but even so, Danglars is able to leave France with over five million francs by embezzling and stealing from various sources, particularly from charity hospitals.

Danglars arrives in Rome, totally unaware that Monte Cristo has informed (1) the banking firm of Thomson and French; (2) Peppino, the person whom Monte Cristo saved earlier from execution; and (3) Luigi Vampa, the Italian bandit who specializes in kidnapping (earlier, he kidnapped Albert de Morcerf). Therefore, when Luigi Vampa kidnaps Danglars and forces him to pay for his food or else starve – 100,000 francs for one chicken – this *demand for money* crucifies Danglars more than would any *physical* pain. Finally, Monte Cristo reveals himself to Danglars: "I am the man you betrayed and dishonored, the man whose fiancée you prostituted, the man on whom you trod on the way to fortune, the man whose father you caused to die of hunger, the man you condemned to die of hunger but who now forgives you because he himself needs to be forgiven. I am Edmond Dantès."

This revelation is too much for Danglars, because when he is released with only a pittance of his fortune remaining, his hair has turned completely white. Now, the Count of Monte Cristo is finally revenged against all of his enemies.

Chapter 73

EPILOGUE

Summary

October has finally come. It is evening. A light yacht is sailing toward a small island, and a tall, dark young man asks if the island ahead of them is the Isle of Monte Cristo. It is, and a shot suddenly flashes loudly from the island. The young man answers it with a shot from his carbine, and ten minutes later, the yacht is anchored, and the young man, Maximilien Morrel, wades ashore, where he is greeted by Monte Cristo.

Maximilien tells the Count that he has come "to die in the arms of a friend who will smile at me during my last moments of life." He fears that his sister, Julie, would burst into tears and that his brother-in-law would snatch his gun away. Clearly, Maximilien is still so morose over Valentine's death that he doesn't want to go on living. In his own words, he has "come to the end of the road," and he can go no further. He checks his watch; he has three more hours to live.

"Come," says the Count, and leads Maximilien to a grotto, which magically becomes a deeply carpeted, underground palace. An odor of sweet, exotic perfume envelops them, while around them, marble statues hold baskets of flowers and fruit. Monte Cristo proposes that the two of them spend Maximilien's last hours "like the ancient Romans."

"No regrets?" he asks Maximilien. "Not even about leaving me?" A tear glistens in Maximilien's eye. Monte Cristo asks him if he isn't afraid of losing his soul, and Maximilien answers that his soul is no longer his own, meaning that it belongs to Valentine. Monte Cristo says that he has long regarded him as a son, but that he hoped for a son who would enjoy life as few people ever could because of untold wealth. "You can have *anything* you want," he tells Maximilien, "Only live!"

But Maximilien is coldly resolute. Only a miracle will save him. Therefore, Monte Cristo goes to a cabinet and takes out a small silver box, in which there is a still smaller golden box, which contains a substance that the Count offers to Maximilien on a spoon. "This is what you asked for, and this is what I promised you," he says. Then he takes a second spoon for himself and dips into the golden box, saying wearily that he too is tired of life.

Maximilien cries out that if the Count were to kill *himself,* it would be a crime, for the Count has faith and hope. Then he quickly bids Monte Cristo farewell, promising to tell Valentine how very good and generous the Count has been to him. He swallows the mysterious substance, and the room suddenly seems to dim, the marble statues become gauzy, and the incense becomes only a whisper. Maximilien thanks Monte Cristo one last time, then he falls lifelessly to the floor. His eyes flicker, and he seems to see a hazy image of Valentine. Is this heaven? Is this death? No sound comes from Maximilien's lips, but his soul cries out to Valentine, and she rushes to him.

"He is calling you," Monte Cristo tells Valentine. "You and Maximilien must never leave one another again. Now I give you back to one another, and may God bless you, and despite all of my acts of vengeance, may He take into account these two lives that I have *saved!"*

Monte Cristo turns to Haydée and tells her that he is entrusting her future to Valentine and Maximilien; but Haydée says that she will die without Monte Cristo. She loves him as she loves life and as she loves God; Monte Cristo is the "finest, the kindest, and the greatest man on this earth!" The Count realizes now that God is, as it were, offering Haydée to him so that he can be happy. He puts his arm around Haydée's waist and leaves, just as Maximilien awakens and is reunited with Valentine.

Next morning at dawn, Jacopo gives Maximilien a note from Monte Cristo. In it, Monte Cristo tells Maximilien that in life, there is neither happiness nor unhappiness. One can only compare one with the other, and one must have suffered terrible despair if one is ever to know ultimate bliss. Both Maximilien and Valentine have known the depths of unhappiness; therefore, they will now know bliss. Monte Cristo asks them both to be happy and to do two things in order to ensure happiness for them: *wait* and *hope.*

On the far horizon, where a hard blue line separates the sky from the Mediterranean, a tiny white sail can be seen. Maximilien bids farewell to Monte Cristo, "my father!," and Valentine bids farewell to Haydée, "my sister!" Then she turns to Maximilien and reminds him that perhaps one day they may see them again – if they only *wait* and *hope,* the two words containing all of human wisdom.

Commentary

Almost every nineteenth-century novel of this period had a final chapter that brought the story to a very neat ending, tidying up all the loose narrative strands. In this final chapter, Monte Cristo puts his beloved young friend Maximilien to a final test to see whether or not his suicide intent is superficial or whether there is indeed the deep love that he suspects. He has held Maximilien in suspense concerning the supposed death of Valentine because "there is neither happiness nor unhappiness in this world; there is only the comparison of one state with another. Only a man who has felt ultimate despair is capable of feeling ultimate bliss." Since Monte Cristo himself felt ultimate despair, we must happily conclude that with his realization of his love for Haydée and Haydée's love for him, that he has at last found "ultimate bliss."

SUGGESTED ESSAY QUESTIONS

1. Consider the four enemies of Edmond Dantès and discuss how the punishment that the Count of Monte Cristo inflicts upon them is related to their deepest ambitions.

2. Using Monte Cristo's concept that great suffering requires prolonged punishment rather than instantaneous death, discuss the justice of the punishment that he inflicts on each of them.

3. Using Albert, Valentine, and Edouard, how does Monte Cristo's theory of "the sins of the fathers must be visited upon subsequent generations" undergo a dramatic reversal?

4. Discuss the metamorphosis of Edmond Dantès from a handsome, naive, and idealistic young man into the sophisticated and aristocratic Count of Monte Cristo.

5. This novel is often considered to be one of the greatest adventure stories in Western literature, yet in reality, it is a novel of intrigue and mystery. Discuss the discrepancy.

SELECT BIBLIOGRAPHY

BASSAN, FERNANDE. *Alexandre Dumas, pere, et la Comedie-Francaise.* Paris: Lettres Modernes, 1972.

BELL, A. CRAIG. *Alexandre Dumas, a Biography and Study.* London: Cassell, 1950.

COOK, MERCER. *Five French Negro Authors.* Washington, D.C.: Associated Publishers, 1943.

GORMAN, HERBERT SHERMAN. *The Incredible Marquis, Alexandre Dumas.* New York: Rinehart, 1929.

HEMMINGS, FREDERICK WILLIAM JOHN. *The King of Romance: A Portrait of Alexandre Dumas.* London, 1929.

LUCAS-DUBRETON, JEAN. *La Vie d'Alexandre Dumas, pere.* Paris: J. Lucas-Dubreton, 1916.

MAUROIS, ANDRE. *Alexandre Dumas: A Great Life in Brief.* New York: Knopf, 1955.

_____. *The Titans.* New York: Hopkins, 1957.

MUNRO, DOUGLAS. *Alexandre Dumas, pere.* New York: Garland, 1981.

PARIGOT, HIPPOLYTE LOUIS. *Alexandre Dumas, pere.* Paris, 1902.

REED, FRANK WILD. *Alexandre Dumas, Benefactor.* New York: Colophon, 1935.

ROSS, MICHAEL. *Alexandre Dumas.* London: Newton Abbot, 1981.

SIMON, G. M. *Histoire d'une Collaboration.* Paris, 1919.

STOWE, RICHARD. *Alexandre Dumas.* New York: Twayne, 1976.

THOMPSON, JOHN A. *Alexandre Dumas, pere, and the Spanish Romance Drama.* Louisiana State University Press, 1938.

NOTES

NOTES

_____
_____
_____
_____
_____
_____
_____
_____
_____
_____
_____
_____
_____
_____
_____
_____
_____
_____
_____
_____
_____
_____
_____